Investigation Procedures and Response

EC-Council | Press

Volume 1 of 5 mapping to

C|HFI™

Computer | Hacking Forensic INVESTIGATOR

Certification

COURSE TECHNOLOGY
CENGAGE Learning™

Australia • Brazil • Japan • Korea • Mexico • Singapore • Spain • United Kingdom • United States

COURSE TECHNOLOGY
CENGAGE Learning™

Investigation Procedures and Response : EC-Council | Press

Course Technology/Cengage Learning Staff:

Vice President, Career and Professional Editorial: Dave Garza

Director of Learning Solutions: Matthew Kane

Executive Editor: Stephen Helba

Managing Editor: Marah Bellegarde

Editorial Assistant: Meghan Orvis

Vice President, Career and Professional Marketing: Jennifer Ann Baker

Marketing Director: Deborah Yarnell

Marketing Manager: Erin Coffin

Marketing Coordinator: Shanna Gibbs

Production Director: Carolyn Miller

Production Manager: Andrew Crouth

Content Project Manager: Brooke Greenhouse

Senior Art Director: Jack Pendleton

EC-Council:

President | EC-Council: Sanjay Bavisi

Sr. Director US | EC-Council: Steven Graham

For product information and technology assistance, contact us at
Cengage Learning Customer & Sales Support, 1-800-354-9706

For permission to use material from this text or product,
submit all requests online at **www.cengage.com/permissions**.
Further permissions questions can be e-mailed to
permissionrequest@cengage.com

Library of Congress Control Number: 2009933547

ISBN-13: 978-1-4354-8349-1

ISBN-10: 1-4354-8349-9

Cengage Learning
5 Maxwell Drive
Clifton Park, NY 12065-2919
USA

Cengage Learning is a leading provider of customized learning solutions with office locations around the globe, including Singapore, the United Kingdom, Australia, Mexico, Brazil, and Japan. Locate your local office at: **international.cengage.com/region**

Cengage Learning products are represented in Canada by Nelson Education, Ltd.

For more learning solutions, please visit our corporate website at **www.cengage.com**

Printed in the United States of America
1 2 3 4 5 6 7 12 11 10 09

Brief Table of Contents

Table of Contents

CHAPTER 3
Computer Investigation Process **3-1**

CHAPTER 6
Investigative Reports 6-1

Hacking and electronic crimes sophistication has grown at an exponential rate in recent years. In fact, recent reports have indicated that cyber crime already surpasses the illegal drug trade! Unethical hackers, better known as *black hats,* are preying on information systems of government, corporate, public, and private networks and are constantly testing the security mechanisms of these organizations to the limit with the sole aim of exploiting them and profiting from the exercise. High-profile crimes have proven that the traditional approach to computer security is simply not sufficient, even with the strongest perimeter, properly configured defense mechanisms such as firewalls, intrusion detection, and prevention systems, strong end-to-end encryption standards, and anti-virus software. Hackers have proven their dedication and ability to systematically penetrate networks all over the world. In some cases, black hats may be able to execute attacks so flawlessly that they can compromise a system, steal everything of value, and completely erase their tracks in less than 20 minutes!

The EC-Council Press is dedicated to stopping hackers in their tracks.

About EC-Council

The International Council of Electronic Commerce Consultants, better known as EC-Council, was founded in late 2001 to address the need for well-educated and certified information security and e-business practitioners. EC-Council is a global, member-based organization comprised of industry and subject matter experts all working together to set the standards and raise the bar in information security certification and education.

EC-Council first developed the *Certified Ethical Hacker* (CIEH) program. The goal of this program is to teach the methodologies, tools, and techniques used by hackers. Leveraging the collective knowledge from hundreds of subject matter experts, the CIEH program has rapidly gained popularity around the globe and is now delivered in more than 70 countries by more than 450 authorized training centers. More than 60,000 information security practitioners have been trained.

CIEH is the benchmark for many government entities and major corporations around the world. Shortly after CIEH was launched, EC-Council developed the *Certified Security Analyst* (EICSA). The goal of the EICSA program is to teach groundbreaking analysis methods that must be applied while conducting advanced penetration testing. The EICSA program leads to the *Licensed Penetration Tester* (LIPT) status. The *Computer Hacking Forensic Investigator* (CIHFI) was formed with the same design methodologies and has become a global standard in certification for computer forensics. EC-Council, through its impervious network of professionals and huge industry following, has developed various other programs in information security and e-business. EC-Council certifications are viewed as the essential certifications needed when standard configuration and security policy courses fall short. Providing a true, hands-on, tactical approach to security, individuals armed with the knowledge disseminated by EC-Council programs are securing networks around the world and beating the hackers at their own game.

About the EC-Council I Press

The EC-Council I Press was formed in late 2008 as a result of a cutting-edge partnership between global information security certification leader, EC-Council and leading global academic publisher, Cengage Learning. This partnership marks a revolution in academic textbooks and courses of study in information security, computer forensics, disaster recovery, and end-user security. By identifying the essential topics and content of EC-Council professional certification programs, and repurposing this world-class content to fit academic programs, the EC-Council I Press was formed. The academic community is now able to incorporate this powerful cutting-edge content into new and existing information security programs. By closing the gap between academic study and professional certification, students and instructors are able to leverage the power of rigorous academic focus and high demand industry certification. The EC-Council I Press is set to revolutionize global information security programs and ultimately create a new breed of practitioners capable of combating the growing epidemic of cybercrime and the rising threat of cyber-war.

Computer Forensics Series

The EC-Council | Press *Computer Forensics* series, preparing learners for C|HFI certification, is intended for those studying to become police investigators and other law enforcement personnel, defense and military personnel, e-business security professionals, systems administrators, legal professionals, banking, insurance and other professionals, government agencies, and IT managers. The content of this program is designed to expose the learner to the process of detecting attacks and collecting evidence in a forensically sound manner with the intent to report crime and prevent future attacks. Advanced techniques in computer investigation and analysis with interest in generating potential legal evidence are included. In full, this series prepares the learner to identify evidence in computer-related crime and abuse cases as well as track the intrusive hacker's path through client system.

Books in Series
- *Computer Forensics: Investigation Procedures and Response/1435483499*
- *Computer Forensics: Investigating Hard Disks, File and Operating Systems/1435483502*
- *Computer Forensics: Investigating Data and Image Files/1435483510*
- *Computer Forensics: Investigating Network Intrusions and Cybercrime/1435483529*
- *Computer Forensics: Investigating Wireless Networks and Devices/1435483537*

Investigation Procedures and Response

The first book in the *Computer Forensics* series is *Investigation Procedures and Response*. Coverage includes a basic understanding of the importance of computer forensics, how to set up a secure lab, the process for forensic investigation including first responder responsibilities, how to handle various incidents and information on the various reports used by computer forensic investigators.

Chapter Contents

Chapter 1, *Computer Forensics in Today's World*, discusses some of the most important problems and concerns forensic investigators face today including objectives and methodologies used in computer forensics. Chapter 2, *Computer Forensic Lab*, describes the physical security needs of a lab and recommends how to maintain security. Chapter 3, *Computer Investigation Process*, introduces the concept of computer investigation and shows the steps involved in investigating computer crime. Chapter 4, *First Responder Procedures*, explains the role of the first responder, how to build a first responder tool-kit and how to avoid some common mistakes often made by first responders. Chapter 5, *Incident Handling*, discusses how to react to various incidents including system crashes, packet flooding, and unauthorized use of another user's account. Chapter 6, *Investigative Reports*, focuses on different investigative reports and how to make sure the report is well-written for use in possible legal matters.

Chapter Features

Many features are included in each chapter and all are designed to enhance the learning experience. Features include:
- *Objectives* begin each chapter and focus the learner on the most important concepts in the chapter.
- *Key Terms* are designed to familiarize the learner with terms that will be used within the chapter.
- *Case Examples,* found throughout the chapter, present short scenarios followed by questions that challenge the learner to arrive at an answer or solution to the problem presented.
- *Chapter Summary*, at the end of each chapter, serves as a review of the key concepts covered in the chapter.
- *Review Questions* allow learners to test their comprehension of the chapter content.
- *Hands-On Projects* encourage learners to apply the knowledge they have gained after finishing the chapter. Files for the Hands-On Projects can be found on the Student Resource Center. Note: You will need your access code provided in your book to enter the site. Visit *www.cengage.com/community/eccouncil* for a link to the Student Resource Center.

Student Resource Center

The Student Resource Center contains all the files you need to complete the Hands-On Projects found at the end of the chapters. Access the Student Resource Center with the access code provided in your book. Visit *www.cengage.com/community/eccouncil* for a link to the Student Resource Center.

Additional Instructor Resources

Free to all instructors who adopt the *Investigation Procedures and Response* book for their courses is a complete package of instructor resources. These resources are available from the Course Technology Web site, *www .cengage.com/coursetechnology*, by going to the product page for this book in the online catalog, and choosing "Instructor Downloads."

Resources include:

- *Instructor Manual* : This manual includes course objectives and additional information to help your instruction.
- *ExamView Testbank*: This Windows-based testing software helps instructors design and administer tests and pre-tests. In addition to generating tests that can be printed and administered, this full-featured program has an online testing component that allows students to take tests at the computer and have their exams automatically graded.
- *PowerPoint Presentations*: This book comes with a set of Microsoft PowerPoint slides for each chapter. These slides are meant to be used as teaching aids for classroom presentations, to be made available to students for chapter reviews, or to be printed for classroom distribution. Instructors are also at liberty to add their own slides.
- *Labs*: These are additional hands-on activities to provide more practice for your students.
- *Assessment Activities*: These are additional assessment opportunities including discussion questions, writing assignments, Internet research activities, and homework assignments along with a final cumulative project.
- *Final Exam*: This exam provides a comprehensive assessment of *Investigation Procedures and Response* content.

Cengage Learning Information Security Community Site

Cengage Learning Information Security Community Site was created for learners and instructors to find out about the latest in information security news and technology.
Visit *community.cengage.com/infosec* to:

- Learn what's new in information security through live news feeds, videos and podcasts;
- Connect with your peers and security experts through blogs and forums;
- Browse our online catalog.

How to Become CIHFI Certified

Today's battles between corporations, governments, and countries are no longer fought only in the typical arenas of boardrooms or battlefields using physical force. Now the battlefield starts in the technical realm, which ties into most every facet of modern day life. The CIHFI certification focuses on the necessary skills to identify an intruder's footprints and to properly gather the necessary evidence to prosecute. The CIHFI certification is primarily targeted at police and other law enforcement personnel, defense and military personnel, e-business security professionals, systems administrators, legal professionals, banking, insurance and other professionals, government agencies, and IT managers. This certification will ensure that you have the knowledge and skills to identify, track, and prosecute the cyber-criminal.

CIHFI certification exams are available through authorized Prometric testing centers. To finalize your certification after your training by taking the certification exam through a Prometric testing center, you must:

1. Apply for and purchase an exam voucher by visiting the EC-Council Press community site: *www.cengage.com/community/eccouncil,* if one was not purchased with your book.
2. Once you have your exam voucher, visit *www.prometric.com* and schedule your exam, using the information on your voucher.
3. Take and pass the CIHFI certification examination with a score of 70% or better.

ClHFI certification exams are also available through Prometric Prime. To finalize your certification after your training by taking the certification exam through Prometric Prime, you must:

1. Purchase an exam voucher by visiting the EC-Council Press Community Site: *www.cengage.com/community/eccouncil*, if one was not purchased with your book.

2. Speak with your instructor about scheduling an exam session, or visit the EC-Council community site referenced above for more information.

3. Take and pass the ClHFI certification examination with a score of 70% or better.

About Our Other EC-Council I Press Products

Ethical Hacking and Countermeasures Series

The EC-Council I Press *Ethical Hacking and Countermeasures* series is intended for those studying to become security officers, auditors, security professionals, site administrators, and anyone who is concerned about or responsible for the integrity of the network infrastructure. The series includes a broad base of topics in offensive network security, ethical hacking, as well as network defense and countermeasures. The content of this series is designed to immerse learners into an interactive environment where they will be shown how to scan, test, hack, and secure information systems. A wide variety of tools, viruses, and malware is presented in these books, providing a complete understanding of the tactics and tools used by hackers. By gaining a thorough understanding of how hackers operate, ethical hackers are able to set up strong countermeasures and defensive systems to protect their organization's critical infrastructure and information. The series, when used in its entirety, helps prepare readers to take and succeed on the ClEH certification exam from EC-Council.

Books in Series
- *Ethical Hacking and Countermeasures: Attack Phases*/143548360X
- *Ethical Hacking and Countermeasures: Threats and Defense Mechanisms*/1435483618
- *Ethical Hacking and Countermeasures: Web Applications and Data Servers*/1435483626
- *Ethical Hacking and Countermeasures: Linux, Macintosh and Mobile Systems*/1435483642
- *Ethical Hacking and Countermeasures: Secure Network Infrastructures*/1435483650

Network Security Administrator Series

The EC-Council I Press *Network Administrator* series, preparing learners for ElNSA certification, is intended for those studying to become system administrators, network administrators, and anyone who is interested in network security technologies. This series is designed to educate learners, from a vendor neutral standpoint, how to defend the networks they manage. This series covers the fundamental skills in evaluating internal and external threats to network security, design, and how to enforce network level security policies, and ultimately protect an organization's information. Covering a broad range of topics from secure network fundamentals, protocols and analysis, standards and policy, hardening infrastructure, to configuring IPS, IDS and firewalls, bastion host and honeypots, among many other topics, learners completing this series will have a full understanding of defensive measures taken to secure their organizations information. The series, when used in its entirety, helps prepare readers to take and succeed on the ElNSA, Network Security Administrator certification exam from EC-Council.

Books in Series
- *Network Defense: Fundamentals and Protocols*/1435483553
- *Network Defense: Security Policy and Threats*/1435483561
- *Network Defense: Perimeter Defense Mechanisms*/143548357X
- *Network Defense: Securing and Troubleshooting Network Operating Systems*/1435483588
- *Network Defense: Security and Vulnerability Assessment*/1435483596

Security Analyst Series

The EC-Council I Press *Security Analyst/Licensed Penetration Tester* series, preparing learners for ElCSA/LPT certification, is intended for those studying to become network server administrators, firewall administrators, security testers, system administrators, and risk assessment professionals. This series covers a broad base of topics in advanced penetration testing and security analysis. The content of this program is designed to expose the learner to groundbreaking methodologies in conducting thorough security analysis, as well as advanced penetration testing techniques. Armed with the knowledge from the *Security Analyst* series, learners will be able to perform the intensive assessments required to effectively identify and mitigate risks to the security of the organizations infrastructure. The series, when used in its entirety, helps prepare readers to take and succeed on the EICSA, Certified Security Analyst, and LIPT, License Penetration Tester certification exam from EC-Council.

Books in Series
- *Certified Security Analyst: Security Analysis and Advanced Tools*/1435483669
- *Certified Security Analyst: Customer Agreements and Reporting Procedures in Security Analysis*/1435483677
- *Certified Security Analyst: Penetration Testing Methodologies in Security Analysis*/1435483685
- *Certified Security Analyst: Network and Communication Testing Procedures in Security Analysis*/1435483693
- *Certified Security Analyst: Network Threat Testing Procedures in Security Analysis*/1435483707

Cyber Safety/1435483715

Cyber Safety is designed for anyone who is interested in learning computer networking and security basics. This product provides information cyber crime; security procedures; how to recognize security threats and attacks, incident response, and how to secure Internet access. This book gives individuals the basic security literacy skills to begin high-end IT programs. The book also prepares readers to take and succeed on the SecurityI5 certification exam from EC-Council.

Wireless Safety/1435483766

Wireless Safety introduces the learner to the basics of wireless technologies and its practical adaptation. *Wireless*I5 is tailored to cater to any individual's desire to learn more about wireless technology. It requires no pre-requisite knowledge and aims to educate the learner in simple applications of these technologies. Topics include wireless signal propagation, IEEE and ETSI wireless standards, WLANs and operation, wireless protocols and communication languages, wireless devices, and wireless security networks. The book also prepares readers to take and succeed on the WirelessI5 certification exam from EC-Council.

Network Safety/1435483774

Network Safety provides the basic core knowledge on how infrastructure enables a working environment. Intended for those in office environments and for home users who want to optimize resource utilization, share infrastructure, and make the best of technology and the convenience it offers. Topics include foundations of networks, networking components, wireless networks, basic hardware components, the networking environment and connectivity as well as troubleshooting. The book also prepares readers to take and succeed on the NetworkI5 certification exam from EC-Council.

Disaster Recovery Professional

The *Disaster Recovery Professional* series, preparing the reader for EIDRP certification, introduces the methods employed in identifying vulnerabilities and how to take the appropriate countermeasures to prevent and mitigate failure risks for an organization. It also provides a foundation in disaster recovery principles, including preparation of a disaster recovery plan, assessment of risks in the enterprise, development of policies, and procedures, and understanding of the roles and relationships of various members of an organization, implementation of the plan, and recovering from a disaster. Students will learn how to create a secure network by putting policies and procedures in place, and how to restore a network in the event of a disaster. The series, when used in its entirety, helps prepare readers to take and succeed on the EIDRP, Disaster Recovery Professional certification exam from EC-Council.

Books in Series
- *Disaster Recovery*/1435488709
- *Business Continuity*/1435488695

Acknowledgements

Michael H. Goldner is the Chair of the School of Information Technology for ITT Technical Institute in Norfolk Virginia, and also teaches bachelor level courses in computer network and information security systems. Michael has served on and chaired ITT Educational Services Inc. National Curriculum Committee on Information Security. He received his Juris Doctorate from Stetson University College of Law, his undergraduate degree from Miami University and has been working for more than 15 years in the area of information technology. He is an active member of the American Bar Association, and has served on that organization's cyber law committee. He is a member of IEEE, ACM, and ISSA, and is the holder of a number of industrially recognized certifications including, CISSP, CEH, CHFI, CEI, MCT, MCSE/Security, Security +, Network +, and A+. Michael recently completed the design and creation of a computer forensic program for ITT Technical Institute and has worked closely with both EC-Council and Delmar/Cengage Learning in the creation of this EC-Council Press series.

Chapter 1

Computer Forensics in Today's World

Objectives

After completing this chapter, you should be able to:

- Understand computer forensics
- Understand the need for computer forensics
- Understand the objectives of computer forensics
- Understand the benefits of forensic readiness
- Understand forensic readiness planning
- Understand cyber crime
- Understand the types of computer crimes
- Understand the key steps in forensic investigations
- Understand the need for forensic investigators
- Understand the enterprise theory of investigation (ETI)
- Understand legal issues involved in computer forensics
- Understand how to report the results of forensic investigations

---

Key Terms

Computer forensics the preservation, identification, extraction, interpretation, and documentation of computer evidence, to include the rules of evidence, legal processes, integrity of evidence, factual reporting of the information found, and providing expert opinion in a court of law or other legal and/or administrative proceeding as to what was found

Cyber crime any illegal act that involves a computer, its systems, or its applications

Enterprise theory of investigation (ETI) a methodology of investigating criminal activity that uses a holistic approach and looks at any criminal activity as a piece of a criminal operation rather than as a single criminal act

Forensic investigator an investigator who helps organizations and law enforcement agencies in investigating cyber crimes and prosecuting the perpetrators of those crimes

Forensic readiness an organization's ability to make optimal use of digital evidence in a limited period of time and with minimal investigation costs; the technical and nontechnical actions that maximize an organization's capability to use digital evidence

Forensic science the application of physical sciences to law in the search for truth in civil, criminal, and social behavioral matters for the purpose of ensuring injustice shall not be done to any member of society

Case Example

Jacob was the vice president of sales for a software giant located in Canada. He was responsible for the growth of the software service sector of his company. He had a team of specialists assisting him in several assignments and signing deals across the globe.

Rachel was a new recruit to Jacob's specialist team. She handled client relations for the software giant. Rachel accused Jacob of demanding sexual favors in return for her annual performance raise. She claimed that Jacob sent a vulgar e-mail in which he made an indecent proposal for the favor if she agreed to his terms. Rachel lodged a complaint against Jacob at the district police department and served a copy of the complaint to the management of the software giant. If found guilty, Jacob faced the possibility of losing his job and reputation, and could have faced up to 3 years of imprisonment as well as a fine of $15,000.

The company management team called Ross, a computer forensic investigator, to determine the truth. Ross searched for e-mails on Rachel's system and found incriminating e-mail from Jacob. Jacob hired an attorney to defend him against the complaint Rachel lodged. Ross produced the evidence before the court of law. James, Jacob's attorney, challenged the evidence Ross had collected. James proved that Ross did not follow chain of custody, and in turn, tampered with the evidence. The court rejected Rachel's case and issued a warning to Ross for tampering with the evidence.

Jacob resigned from his post, even though the allegations were proved false, and started his own software service company.

Introduction to Computer Forensics in Today's World

The field of computer investigations and forensics is still in its developing stages. This chapter focuses on computer forensics in today's world. It discusses some of the most important problems and concerns that forensic investigators face today. It first presents the evolution of computer forensics and explains forensic science and computer forensics. It then discusses the need for computer forensics and the objectives and methodologies used therein. The chapter then covers aspects of organization security, forensic readiness, and cyber crime. It concludes by explaining cyber crime investigations.

Evolution of Computer Forensics

- **1888:** Francis Galton made the first-ever recorded study of fingerprints to catch potential criminals in crimes such as murders.

- **1893:** Hans Gross was the first person to apply science to a criminal investigation.

- **1910:** Albert Osborn became the first person to develop the essential features of documenting evidence during the examination process.

- **1915:** Leone Lattes was the first person to use blood groupings to connect criminals to a crime.

- **1925:** Calvin Goddard became the first person to make use of firearms and bullet comparisons for solving many pending court cases.

- **1932:** The Federal Bureau of Investigation (FBI) set up a laboratory to provide forensic services to all field agents and other law authorities.

- **1984:** The Computer Analysis and Response Team (CART) was developed to provide support to FBI field offices searching for computer evidence.

- **1993:** The first international conference on computer evidence was held in the United States.

- **1995:** The International Organization on Computer Evidence (IOCE) was formed to provide a forum to global law enforcement agencies for exchanging information regarding cyber crime investigations and other issues associated with computer forensics.
- **1998:** The International Forensic Science Symposium was formed to provide a forum for forensic managers and to exchange information.
- **2000:** The first FBI Regional Computer Forensic Laboratory (RCFL) was established for the examination of digital evidence in support of criminal investigations such as identity theft, hacking, computer viruses, terrorism, investment fraud, cyber stalking, drug trafficking, phishing/spoofing, wrongful programming, credit card fraud, online auction fraud, e-mail bombing and spam, and property crime.

Forensic Science

According to the *Handbook of Forensic Pathology* prepared by the College of American Pathologists, *forensic science* is defined as the "application of physical sciences to law in the search for truth in civil, criminal, and social behavioral matters to the end that injustice shall not be done to any member of the society."

The main aim of any forensic investigation is to determine the evidential value of the crime scene and the related evidence. Forensic scientists properly analyze the physical evidence, provide expert testimony in court, and furnish training in the proper recognition, collection, and preservation of physical evidence.

Computer Forensics

According to Steve Hailey of the CyberSecurity Institute, *computer forensics* is "the preservation, identification, extraction, interpretation, and documentation of computer evidence, to include the rules of evidence, legal processes, integrity of evidence, factual reporting of the information found, and providing expert opinion in a court of law or other legal and/or administrative proceeding as to what was found."

Need for Computer Forensics

The need for computer forensics has become more apparent with the exponential increase in the number of cyber crimes and litigations in which large organizations are involved. It has become a necessity for organizations to either employ the services of a computer forensic agency or hire a computer forensic expert in order to protect the organization from computer incidents or solve cases involving the use of computers and related technologies. The staggering financial losses caused as a result of computer crimes have also contributed to a renewed interest in computer forensics.

Computer forensics offers the following benefits to organizations:

- Ensures the overall integrity and continued existence of an organization's computer system and network infrastructure.
- Helps the organization capture important information if their computer systems or networks are compromised. It also helps prosecute the case, if the criminal is caught.
- Extracts, processes, and interprets the actual evidence in order to prove the attacker's actions and the organization's innocence in court.
- Efficiently tracks down cyber criminals and terrorists from different parts of the world. Cyber criminals and terrorists that use the Internet as a communication medium can be tracked down and their plans known. IP addresses play a vital role in determining the geographical position of terrorists.
- Saves the organization money and valuable time. Many managers allocate a large portion of their IT budget for computer and network security.
- Tracks complicated cases such as child pornography and e-mail spamming.

A computer forensic expert ensures that the following rules are upheld during an investigation:

- No possible evidence is damaged, destroyed, or compromised by the forensic procedures used to investigate the computer (preservation of evidence).
- No possible computer malware is introduced to the computer being investigated during the analysis process (prevention of contamination of evidence).

- Any extracted and possibly relevant evidence is properly handled and protected from later mechanical or electromagnetic damage (extraction and preservation of evidence).

- A continuing chain of custody is established and maintained (accountability of evidence).

- Normal operations are affected for a limited period of time, if at all (limited interference of the crime scene on normal life).

- Details of the client-attorney relationship are not disclosed if obtained during a forensic process in order to maintain professional ethics and legality (ethics of investigation).

Objectives of Computer Forensics

The overall objective of all computer forensic phases (preservation, identification, extraction, interpretation, and documentation) is to detect a computer incident, identify the intruder, and prosecute the perpetrator in a court of law. With an increase in computer crime incidents ranging from theft of intellectual property to cyber terrorism, the objectives of computer crimes are becoming more pervasive in nature.

The main objectives of computer forensics can be summarized as follows:

- To recover, analyze, and preserve the computer and related materials in a manner that can be presented as evidence in a court of law

- To identify the evidence in a short amount of time, estimate the potential impact of the malicious activity on the victim, and assess the intent and identity of the perpetrator

Computer Forensic Methodologies

Computer forensic tools and methodologies are major components of an organization's disaster recovery preparedness and play a decisive role in overcoming and tackling computer incidents. Due to the growing misuse of computers in criminal activities, there must be a proper set of methodologies to use in an investigation. The evidence acquired from computers is fragile and can be easily erased or altered, and the seized computer can be compromised if not handled using proper methodologies. The methodologies involved in computer forensics may differ depending upon the procedures, resources, and target company.

Forensic tools enable the forensic examiner to recover deleted files, hidden files, and temporary data that the user may not locate.

A forensic investigator must focus on fundamental areas such as standalone computers, workstations, servers, and online channels. Investigation of standalone computers, workstations, and other removable media can be simple. Examination of servers and online channels, however, can be complicated and tricky.

During investigations, logs are often not examined or audited. The investigator must realize that logs play a key role during investigations. They must be given due importance, as they could provide a lead in the case.

Computer forensic methodologies consist of the following basic activities:

- *Preservation*: The forensic investigator must preserve the integrity of the original evidence. The original evidence should not be modified or damaged. The forensic examiner must make an image or a copy of the original evidence and then perform the analysis on that image or copy. The examiner must also compare the copy with the original evidence to identify any modifications or damage.

- *Identification*: Before starting the investigation, the forensic examiner must identify the evidence and its location. For example, evidence may be contained in hard disks, removable media, or log files. Every forensic examiner must understand the difference between actual evidence and evidence containers. Locating and identifying information and data is a challenge for the digital forensic investigator. Various examination processes such as keyword searches, log file analyses, and system checks help an investigation.

- *Extraction*: After identifying the evidence, the examiner must extract data from it. Since volatile data can be lost at any point, the forensic investigator must extract this data from the copy made from the original evidence. This extracted data must be compared with the original evidence and analyzed.

- *Interpretation*: The most important role a forensic examiner plays during investigations is to interpret what he or she has actually found. The analysis and inspection of the evidence must be interpreted in a lucid manner.

- *Documentation*: From the beginning of the investigation until the end (when the evidence is presented before a court of law), forensic examiners must maintain documentation relating to the evidence. The documentation comprises the chain of custody form and documents relating to the evidence analysis.

	Small (<50 staff)	Large (>250 staff)	Very Large (>500 staff)
Companies that had a security incident in the last year	45%	72%	96%
Average number of incidents, median (mean)	6 (100)	15 (200)	>400 (>1,300)
Average cost of worst incident in year	$10k to $20k	$90k to $170k	$1m to $2m

Figure 1-1 This shows the number of companies that reported a security breach, according to a 2008 survey.

Broad Tests for Evidence

After the evidence is collected, investigators perform general tests on the evidence (utilizing both computer forensics as well as generic forensics) to determine the following:

1. *Authenticity*: The investigator must determine the source of the evidence.
2. *Reliability*: The investigator must determine if the evidence is reliable and flawless.

Security Incidents

Organizations, irrespective of their size, use the Internet for their IT activities. According to industry reports, in the near future more than 30% of organizations will be using VoIP (Voice over Internet Protocol) technologies for their business communications. Currently, about 11% of all phone calls worldwide use VoIP at some point in the connection, with some analysts forecasting a $10 billion a year business for broadband providers selling a majority of the world's phone calls. This increase in Internet IT activities brings with it an increase in cyber crime activities.

For example, the Department for Business, Enterprise & Regulatory Reform in the U.K. conducted an information security breach survey in 2008. According to the survey report, 96% of big business detected security breaches. The report estimated that the United Kingdom lost up to $3.7 million in 2007 to cyber crime. Additionally, more than 72% of large companies (> 250 staff) detected security breaches and lost up to $170k.

Figure 1-1 displays the number of companies that reported a security breach in the security breach survey.

How Serious Were the Different Types of Incidents?

The rapid increase in information technology and wide usage of the Internet has caused computer crimes to grow faster and to include international dimensions. Every day a new crime is committed with complex jurisdictional issues.

Figure 1-2 shows the responses given in the Department for Business, Enterprise & Regulatory Reform in the U.K.'s 2008 security breach survey, when organizations were asked about the seriousness of the various reported computer crime incidents.

Incidents Disrupting Business

According to the survey conducted by the Department for Business, Enterprise & Regulatory Reform (BERR), half of the most horrible incidents reported disrupted the business. For example, denial-of-service attacks caused major disruption to medium-sized financial organizations. Malicious software attacks, system failures, or attacks on Web sites caused major disruptions to businesses as well.

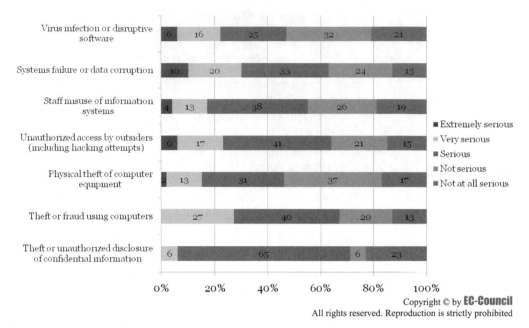

Figure 1-2 This shows the seriousness of reported computer crime incidents, according to a 2008 survey.

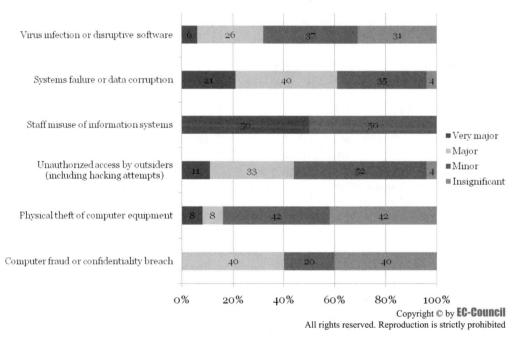

Figure 1-3 This shows the disruptive computer crime incidents reported in the security breach survey.

Figure 1-3 shows the computer crime incidents that were most disruptive to the businesses, based on the responses obtained from the survey.

The time required to respond to each security incident varies based on the type and seriousness of the computer crime. For example, in cases that involve the staff misuse of information systems, the forensic investigation requires a search warrant and legal proceeding, which takes more staff time. In the case of a system failure and data corruption, most of the time is spent restoring the system and fixing the problem.

Figure 1-4 shows the time staff spent responding to various security incidents.

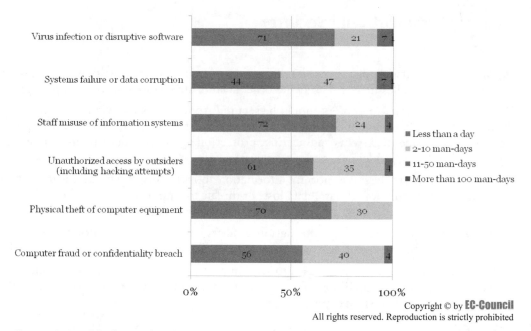

Figure 1-4 This shows the time spent responding to the security incidents, according to a 2008 survey.

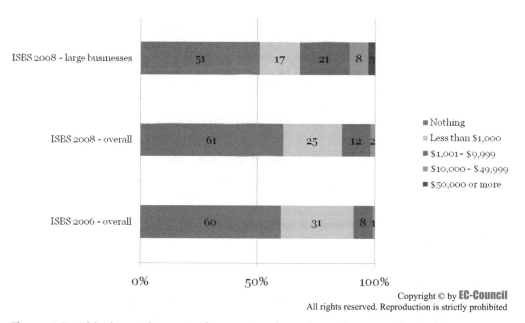

Figure 1-5 This shows the costs of recovering from the various security incidents.

Costs of Responding to Security Incidents

Figure 1-5 shows the costs associated with responding to the various security incidents.

Any information technology system, by its very nature, is vulnerable to attack by criminals. Information security methodologies must be used to mitigate these risks and protect organizations from these cyber crime activities.

Aspects of Organizational Security

IT Security

- *Application security*: Applications should be secured to overcome security weaknesses, vulnerabilities, and threats. Any loopholes in Web-based and other custom applications serve as opportunities for attackers.

- *Computing security*: Computers should be secured from threats like viruses, Trojans, and intruders. To have an effective business operation, organizations must have an effective security policy which involves security management, systems engineering, protection against insider threats, and general workplace policies, standards, guidelines, and procedures.

- *Data security*: Data refers to important information about the organization. It is important to secure data to avoid any manipulation of data, data loss, or threats to data secrecy. Any change in the identity of data or any loss of data causes a huge amount of damage, financial loss, and loss of goodwill for the organization.

- *Information security*: Securing information protects information and information systems from illegal access, use, modification, or destruction. It ensures confidentiality, integrity, and availability of data.

- *Network security*: Networks are used to send important and private data from one system to another. Networks should be secured for safe transfer of data. Damage to the network makes the data transfer vulnerable and may crash the system.

Physical Security

- *Facilities security*: Facilities and an organization's equipment should be properly and highly secured. Damage to facilities can cause physical harm such as a system crash or power failure.

- *Human security*: The employees of an organization should be given security awareness training and be involved in the entire business security process in order to gain their trust and acceptance of the security policy. Ignoring human security concerns can cause employees to leave, leading to loss of business.

Financial Security

- *Security from fraud*: To function properly and negate losses, an organization must be financially secure from both internal and external threats. Security breaches may be caused by data manipulations, system vulnerabilities and threats, or data theft.

Legal Security

- *National security*: National security is threatened if there are any governmental problems, improper management, economic slowdown, or other nationwide issues.

- *Public security*: Public security is threatened if there are any internal riots, strikes, or clashes among the people of the country.

Forensic Readiness

Forensic readiness involves an organization having specific incident response procedures in place, with designated trained personnel assigned to handle any investigation. It enables an organization to collect and preserve digital evidence in a quick and efficient manner with minimal investigation costs. Forensic readiness combined with an enforceable security policy also helps to mitigate the risk of threat from employees. It is part of preemptive measures that every organization should have in place. For example, a warning banner such as "Your actions are being monitored" eliminates any expectation of privacy and cautions the employee against inappropriate activity, intentional or inadvertent. Having an incident response team that is forensically trained and ready ensures that proper procedures are followed and that any evidence of wrongdoing will be handled according to proper legal procedure for possible use in a court of law.

Having an incident response team that is forensically ready can offer an organization the following benefits:

- Evidence can be accumulated to act in the company's defense if subject to a lawsuit.

- Comprehensive evidence collection can be used as a deterrent to insider threat and can assure that no important evidence is overlooked.

- In the event of a major incident, a fast and efficient investigation can be conducted and corresponding actions can be taken with minimal disruption to day-to-day business activity.

- A fixed and structured approach for storage of evidence can considerably reduce the expenses and time of an internal investigation while preserving the all-important chain of custody.

- A structured approach to storage of all digital information can not only reduce the costs of any court-ordered disclosure or regulatory/legal need to disclose data, but is now a requirement under federal law (e.g., in response to a request for discovery under the Federal Rules of Civil Procedure).

- The protection offered by an information security policy can be extended to cover wider threats of cyber crime, such as intellectual property protection, fraud, or extortion.

- It demonstrates due diligence and good corporate governance of the company's information assets, as measured by the "Reasonable Man" standard.

- It can demonstrate that regulatory requirements have been met.

- It can improve upon and make the interface to law enforcement easier.

- It can improve the prospects of successful legal action.

- It can provide evidence to resolve commercial or privacy disputes.

- It can support employee sanctions up to and including termination based on digital evidence (e.g., to prove violation of an acceptable-use policy).

Goals of Forensic Readiness

The main goal of any forensic investigation is the collection of digital evidence. The main focus of forensic readiness is to support the organization's prerequisite need to use digital evidence in its defense in some matter. A forensic readiness approach consists of both technical and nontechnical procedures that maximize an organization's capability to use digital evidence to mitigate risk, protect against cyber crime attacks, and prosecute wrongs.

Forensic readiness strives to meet the following goals:

- To collect critical evidence in a forensically sound manner without unduly interfering with normal business processes

- To gather evidence demonstrating possible criminal activity or disputes that may adversely impact an organization

- To allow an investigation to proceed while keeping cost proportional to the cost of the incident

- To ensure that any evidence collected can have a positive effect on the outcome of any legal proceeding

Forensic Readiness Planning

The following steps describe the key activities in forensic readiness planning:

1. *Define the business scenarios that might require the collection of digital evidence.*

   The first step in forensic readiness is to define the purpose of an evidence collection capability. The rationale is to look at the risk and potential impact on the business from various criminal activities and disputes. What is the threat to the business and what assets are vulnerable to the defined threats? This process is known as risk assessment and follows a defined procedure at the enterprise level to mitigate any potential risks to the organization. One of the principal functions of risk assessment is to understand the business scenarios in which digital evidence may be required and may benefit the organization in the event it is required. Areas where the forensic readiness process may be applied include:

   - Reducing the impact of computer-related crime
   - Dealing effectively with court orders to collect and release data
   - Demonstrating compliance with regulatory or legal constraints
   - Producing evidence to support company disciplinary issues
   - Supporting contractual and commercial agreements
   - Proving the impact of a crime or dispute on the organization

2. *Identify the potential available evidence.*

The second step in a forensic readiness program is for an organization to know what sources of potential evidence are present on, or could be generated by, its systems. It must also determine what currently happens to the potential evidence data. Computer logs can originate from many sources. The purpose of this step is to see what evidence may be available from across the range of systems and applications in use.

3. *Determine the evidence collection requirement.*

At this point, enough information is available to determine which evidence sources identified in Step 2 can help in dealing with the crimes and disputes identified in Step 1. Additionally, the best methods to collect the indicated evidence must be designated. This is an evidence collection requirement.

The purpose of this step is to produce an evidence requirement statement allowing those responsible for managing the business risk to communicate with those running and monitoring information systems through an agreed-upon requirement for incident response and evidence collection.

One of the key benefits of this step is applying IT to the corporate security needs. IT audit logs have been traditionally configured by system administrators independently of corporate policy. Often where such a policy exists, there is a significant gap between organizational security objectives and the bottom-up auditing actually being implemented.

4. *Designate procedures for securely collecting evidence that meets the defined requirement in a forensically acceptable manner.*

At this point, the organization knows the totality of available evidence and has decided what can be collected to address the company risks within a planned budget. With the evidence requirement understood, the next step is to ensure that the evidence is collected from the relevant sources and is preserved as both an authentic record and part of normal business activity.

Legal advice should be received to ensure that the evidence can be gathered legally and the evidence requirement can be met as outlined in the security policy. For example; does it involve monitoring personal e-mails, the use of personal data, or just general spying on employee activities without valid reasons? In some countries, some or all of these activities may be illegal. Relevant laws in the areas of data protection, privacy, and human rights will inevitably constrain what can actually be gathered.

5. *Establish a policy for securely handling and storing the collected evidence.*

All digitally stored information being collected for use as possible evidence must be secure for the long term and available for retrieval if it is required at a later date.

A policy for secure storage and handling of potential evidence comprises security measures to ensure the authenticity of the data and procedures to demonstrate that the evidence integrity is preserved whenever it is accessed, used, moved, or combined with additional digital information. In the parlance of investigators, this is known as continuity of evidence in the United Kingdom and chain of custody in the United States. The continuity of evidence also includes records of who held and who had access to the evidence (for example, from swipe-control door logs).

The required output of this step is a secure evidence policy. It should document the security measures, the legal advice, and the procedural measures used to ensure that the evidence requirement is met. The likely admissibility and weight of any evidence gathered rests upon this document.

6. *Ensure that the monitoring process is designed to detect and prevent unexpected or adverse incidents.*

In addition to gathering evidence for later use in court, evidence sources can be monitored to detect threatened incidents in a timely manner and minimize the negative effects to the business organization. For example, intrusion detection systems (IDS) extend beyond network attacks to a wide range of behaviors that may have implications for the organization. By monitoring sources of evidence, investigators can look for triggers which imply that something suspicious may be happening.

The critical question in this step is, when should an organization be suspicious? A suspicious event has to be related to business risk and not just explained in technical terms. Thus, the onus is on managers to explain to those monitoring the data what they want to prevent, thus setting the threshold at which activity becomes suspicious. This threshold describes the sort of behavior that an IDS might use to detect an incident. This should be established in the section of the security policy procedures that helps the various monitoring and auditing staff understand what triggers should provoke suspicion, who to report the suspicion to, whether heightened monitoring is required, and whether any additional security measures should be taken to mitigate and prevent further intrusion or damage.

Each type of monitoring will produce a proportion of false positives. The sensitivity of triggers can be varied as long as the overall false-positive rate does not become so high that suspicious events cannot be properly reviewed. Varying triggers also guard against the risk of someone aware of the threshold level on a particular event making sure that any events or transactions he or she wishes to hide are beneath it.

7. *Ensure investigative staff members are properly trained and capable of completing any task related to evidence collection and preservation.*

A wide range of staff may become involved in a computer security incident. This process ensures that appropriate training is provided to assist staff for the various roles they may play before, during, and after an incident. It is also necessary to ensure that staff members are competent to perform any roles related to the handling and preservation of evidence.

There will be some issues relevant to all staff involved in an incident. For example, the following groups will require more specialized awareness training:

- The investigating team
- Corporate HR department
- Corporate PR department
- Owners of business processes or data
- Line management and profit-center managers
- Corporate security
- System administrators
- IT management
- Legal advisers
- Senior management

8. *Create step-by-step documentation of all activities performed and their impact.*

The purpose of this step is to produce a policy that describes how an evidence-based case should be assembled. A case file may be required for a number of reasons:

- Provide a basis for interaction with legal advisers and law enforcement
- Support a report to a regulatory body
- Support an insurance claim
- Justify disciplinary action
- Provide feedback on how such an incident can be avoided in the future
- Provide a record in case of a similar event in the future
- Provide further evidence if required in the future (for example, if no action is deemed necessary at this point but further developments occur)

9. *Ensure authorized review to facilitate action in response to the incident.*

At certain points during the collating of the cyber crime case file, it will be necessary to review the case from a legal standpoint and receive legal advice on any follow-up actions. Legal advisers should be able to offer advice on the strength of the case and suggest whether additional measures should be taken. For example, if the evidence is weak, is it necessary to catch an internal suspect "red-handed" by monitoring his or her activity and seizing his or her PC? Caution should be used here as some illegal activity can require the immediate involvement of law enforcement.

Therefore, any escalation to a formal action will need to be justified, cost effective, and approved, ensuring it will be more likely to end in the company's favor. Although the actual decision about how to proceed will clearly be made after the incident, considerable legal preparation is required in readiness.

Legal advisers should be trained and experienced in the appropriate cyber laws and evidence admissibility issues. They must be prepared to act on an incident pursuant to the digital evidence that has been gathered and the case presented in Step 8. Legal advisers should also recognize that the legal issues may span national and/or international legal jurisdictions. Advice from legal advisers should include:

- Any liabilities from the incident and how they can be managed
- Finding and prosecuting/punishing (internal versus external culprits)

- Legal and regulatory constraints on what action can be taken
- Reputation protection and PR issues
- When/if to advise partners, customers, and investors
- How to deal with employees
- Resolving commercial disputes
- Any additional measures required

Cyber Crime

Cyber crime is defined as "any illegal act that involves a computer, its systems, or its applications." Cyber crimes are intentional. Cyber criminals have become more organized than in the past and are considered more technically advanced than the agencies that plan to thwart them.

Cyber crimes are generally categorized by the following information:

- *Tools of the crime*: The tools of the crime are the evidence that the forensic investigator must analyze, process, and document. This may include various hacking tools used to commit the crime or the computer/workstation where the crime was committed. Forensic investigators usually take the entire system used, including hardware such as the keyboard, mouse, and monitor.
- *Target of the crime*: The target of the crime is the victim. The victim is most often a corporate organization, Web site, consulting agency, or government body. The target of the crime is also usually where the computer forensic investigator examines the crime scene. Since investigators are mainly dealing with digital rather than physical, this can often be a virtual environment.

Cyber crimes include the following:

- Crimes directed against a computer
- Crimes in which the computer contains evidence
- Crimes in which the computer is used as a tool to commit the crime

Computer-Facilitated Crimes

Although the first computer crime was reported in 1969, today's computer crimes pose new challenges for investigators due to their speed, anonymity, and the fleeting nature of evidence.

Dependence on the computer has given way to new crimes in which the computer is used as a tool for committing crimes. Computers can facilitate crimes such as spamming, corporate espionage, identity theft, writing or spreading computer viruses and worms, denial-of-service attacks, distribution of pornography, cyber theft, hacking, data-transfer theft, and software piracy.

Modes of Attacks

Two modes of attack are used in cyber crimes insider attacks and external attacks.

Insider Attacks

The primary threat to computer systems has traditionally been the insider attack. An insider attack occurs when there is a breach of trust from employees within the organization. Insiders are likely to have specific goals and objectives, and have legitimate access to the system. Insiders can plant Trojan horses or browse through the file system. This type of attack can be extremely difficult to detect or to protect against.

The insider attack can affect all components of computer security. Browsing attacks the confidentiality of information on the system. Trojan horses are a threat to both the integrity and confidentiality of the system. Insiders can affect availability by overloading the system's processing or storage capacity, or by causing the system to crash.

Insider attacks usually cost companies millions of dollars. It is difficult for the organization's senior management to know which one of the employees is snooping the networks for any weaknesses. Insider attacks often occur without warning. Figure 1-6 shows how an internal attack is executed.

Many system and network administrators presume that the network is safe from any attack within the organization. Therefore, they go about fortifying the network with suitable firewalls to keep intruders at bay. However, these firewalls do nothing to protect the network against insider attacks.

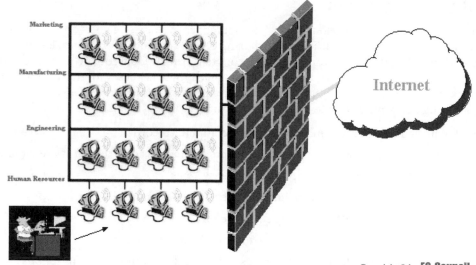

Figure 1-6 Insider attacks occur when there is a breach of trust by employees within the organization.

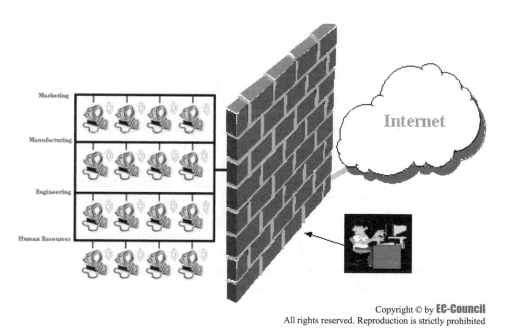

Figure 1-7 External attacks originate from outside of an organization.

External Attacks

External attacks are due to poor information security policies and procedures. These types of attacks originate from outside of an organization. The attacker is either hired by an insider or an external entity to destroy a competitor's reputation. According to various security reports a company is targeted, on average, for intrusions every 15 minutes from some outside source. Due to the large number of attempts, it becomes difficult to track down and prosecute the suspect of an external attack. The suspect may even be operating from a machine that is across the world. Figure 1-7 shows how an external attack is conducted.

Examples of Cyber Crime

Cyber crime involves illegal exploitation of computer technologies. Cyber crimes usually use the Internet to commit crimes such as fraud, identity theft, sharing of information, and embezzlement.

Exactly what is illegal varies greatly from territory to territory. Consequently, the growth of international data communications and, in particular, the Internet has made these crimes both more common and more difficult to police. Luckily there are people fighting computer crime, and it is taken seriously by government agencies.

The following are some examples of computer crime:

- Fraud achieved through the manipulation of computer records
- Spamming where outlawed completely or where regulations controlling it are violated
- Deliberate circumvention of computer security systems
- Unauthorized access to or modification of software programs
- Intellectual property theft, including software piracy
- Industrial espionage by means of access to or theft of computer materials
- Identity theft accomplished through the use of fraudulent computer transactions
- Writing or spreading computer viruses or worms
- "Salami slicing," which is the practice of stealing money repeatedly in small quantities
- Denial-of-service attacks, in which company Web sites are flooded with service requests and overloaded, and are either slowed or crashed completely
- Making and digitally distributing child pornography

Types of Computer Crimes

The following are some types of computer crimes:

- *Identity theft*: According to the U.S. Department of Justice (USDOJ), identity theft refers to all types of crime in which someone wrongfully obtains and uses another person's personal data in a way that involves fraud or deception, typically for economic gain. Common forms of identity theft are shoulder surfing, dumpster diving, spamming, spoofing, phishing, and skimming. The criminal steals a person's identity by stealing e-mail, information from computer databases, or eavesdropping on transactions over the Internet.

- *Hacking*: Hacking is a practice used to obtain illegal access to computer systems owned by private corporations or government agencies in order to modify computer hardware and software. People who are involved in hacking are often referred to as hackers.

- *Computer viruses and worms*: Viruses and worms are software programs with malicious code. These programs are designed to spread from one computer to another. Viruses can affect machines and seek to affect other vulnerable systems through applications such as an e-mail client. Worms seek to replicate themselves over the network, thereby exhausting resources and creating malfunctions. Trojan horses and backdoors are programs that allow an intruder to retain access to a compromised machine.

- *Cyber stalking*: Cyber stalking is any ominous or improper behavior where cyber criminals use the Internet and other communication methods to victimize people. With the easy availability of computers and online services, cyber stalkers can collect personal information about the victim through e-mails, chat rooms, message boards, and discussion forums, and then make unwanted advances toward and harass the victim.

- *Cyber bullying*: This is similar to cyber stalking, but usually refers to the aggressive or bullying behavior of juveniles.

- *Drug trafficking*: Drug trafficking refers to selling illegal substances over the Internet with the help of encrypted e-mails. Drug traffickers take advantage of Internet technologies such as Internet cafés and courier Web sites to sell illegal substances.

- *Program manipulation fraud*: Program manipulation fraud involves a perpetrator changing existing computer programs by either modifying them or inserting new programs and routines. The Trojan horse is one common method that cyber criminals use to manipulate programs.

- *Credit card fraud*: Credit card fraud involves the unauthorized use of another person's credit card information for the purpose of either charging purchases to or removing funds from the victim's account. It is a form of identity theft.

- *Financial fraud*: Financial fraud is any criminal behavior in which a person uses fraudulent methods to trick a victim out of his or her money. One of the most common examples of financial fraud is the Internet fraud scheme. Internet fraud schemes involve emulated online auctions, retail schemes, business opportunity schemes, identity theft, market manipulation schemes, and credit card schemes.

- *Online auction fraud*: Online auctions make purchasing easy if the vendor is trusted. However, fraudulent techniques are often used to deceive the customer. According to the Internet Crime Complaint Center (IC3), online auction fraud involves the following:

  - Misrepresentation of product or manufactured goods advertised for sale through online auction Web sites

  - Nondelivery of an item purchased through online auction Web sites

- *E-mail bombing and spamming*: E-mail bombing refers to a technique abusers use that repeatedly sends an e-mail message to a particular address at a specific victim's site. E-mail spamming involves abusers sending e-mail (junk mail) to hundreds or even thousands of users. E-mail bombing/spamming may be integrated with e-mail spoofing, making it difficult to determine who actually sent the e-mail.

- *Theft of intellectual property*: Intellectual property thefts include any acts that would allow individuals to gain access to patents, trade secrets, customer data, sales trends, and any other confidential information that can be of monetary gain. For example, if an individual were to get access to trade secrets of a particular organization and were to sell this information to a rival company, it would be considered a crime. Losses incurred by companies due to this crime can range from $100 to $1,000,000, depending on the size of the company.

- *Denial-of-service (DoS) attacks*: DoS attacks are the most common attacks employed against company networks. DoS attacks aim at stopping legitimate requests to a network over the Internet by subjecting the network to illegitimate requests. DoS attacks occur when several systems take up useful network resources, thereby rendering the network inaccessible.

- *Debt elimination*: According to the IC3, debt elimination schemes generally involve Web sites advertising a legal way to dispose of mortgage loans and credit card debts. The participant discloses personal details as well as information related to the loans, and scammers then commit identity theft crimes by using the personal information to benefit themselves.

- *Webjacking*: In this type of attack, hackers or attackers gain unauthorized access to and control over Web sites, and change the information on Web sites.

- *Internet extortion*: Internet extortion is obtaining something from a person by threatening to cause harm to him or her and is often monetary in nature. According to IC3, Internet extortion involves hacking into and controlling various industry databases, promising to release control back to the company if funds are received or the subjects are given Web administrator jobs. The subject will threaten to compromise information about consumers in the industry database unless funds are received.

- *Investment fraud*: According to IC3, investment fraud is an offer using false or fraudulent claims to solicit investments or loans, or providing for the purchase, use, or trade of forged or counterfeit securities. This often results in a loss to the investors.

- *Escrow services fraud*: According to IC3, in an effort to persuade a wary Internet auction participant, the perpetrator of escrow services fraud will propose the use of a third-party escrow service to facilitate the exchange of money and merchandise. The victim is unaware the perpetrator has actually compromised a true escrow site and, in actuality, created one that closely resembles a legitimate escrow service. The victim sends payment to the phony escrow and receives nothing in return. Alternately, the victim sends merchandise to the perpetrator and waits for his or her payment through the escrow site. The payment is never received, however, because it is not a legitimate service.

- *Cyber defamation*: Cyber defamation is an act of defaming a person, Web site, or organization on the Internet. Cyber defamation develops a false reputation and hatred among people.

- *Software piracy*: Software piracy is the unauthorized copying or uploading of software, music, or movies from the Internet with the intent to sell the copied items. Piracy is illegal and perpetrators can be convicted under copyright law.

- *Counterfeit cashier's checks*: The counterfeit cashier's check scam is a nasty scheme that hinges on people's long-standing belief that a cashier's check is as good as gold.

     In this type of scam, people are contacted by e-mail or regular mail, even if they aren't selling online. The correspondence could mention a sweepstakes prize or lottery, claiming that the victim has won a huge prize. The letter states that the sweepstakes or lottery organization will send the victim a cashier's check, but he or she has to send the organization funds to cover the processing fee beforehand. There are endless variations of this particular scam.

- *Damage to company service networks*: Either insiders or outsiders can damage company service networks. An attacker can plant a Trojan horse, conduct a denial-of-service attack, and install an unauthorized modem in the network to allow outsiders to gain access. These attacks usually take place when there is a breach of security policies and acceptable-use measures.

- *Embezzlement*: Embezzlement is defined as "the fraudulent conversion of property of another by a person in lawful possession of that property." Crimes of this nature generally have involved a relationship of trust and confidence, such as an agent, fiduciary, trustee, treasurer, or attorney.

- *Copyright piracy*: Copyright is a form of protection provided by the laws of the United States (title 17, U. S. Code) to the authors of original works, including literary, dramatic, musical, artistic, and certain other intellectual works. Cyber criminals often upload copyrighted works to the Internet making them available to other users, often for a fee.

- *Child pornography*: Child pornography refers to the sexual exploitation or abuse of a child. It can be defined as any means of depicting or promoting the sexual exploitation of a child including written, audio, or video material which focuses on the child's sexual behavior or genitals. The Internet provides a means for child pornographers to both find children to exploit and to share pornographic material with others.

- *Password trafficking*: Passwords are a standard measure of security for individual accounts while accessing computers and performing Internet-based transactions. Passwords are generally limited to individuals. To illegally access such accounts, an intruder adopts certain methods to steal passwords without being detected. The law targets illegal acquisition of passwords. According to U.S. Code 18, two conditions trigger an offense:

  - The trafficking must affect interstate or foreign commerce
  - The computer is used by or for the U. S. government

  Minimum penalties may include fines, imprisonment for up to one year, or both.

- *Hacker system penetrations*: A network or system penetration occurs when an outsider gets access to a network and changes settings within it. These attacks can occur through Trojans, rootkits, and the use of sniffers and other tools that take advantage of vulnerabilities in network security.

- *Telecommunications crime*: Telecommunications crimes include unauthorized access to telephone systems, cloning cellular telephones, intercepting communications, and creating false communications.

Cyber Crime Investigations

The investigation of any crime involves the painstaking collection of clues and forensic evidence with an attention to detail. These methods are even more important in white-collar crimes where documentary evidence plays a crucial role. With an increasing number of households and businesses using computers, coupled with easy Internet access, it is inevitable that there will be at least one electronic device found during the investigation. This may be a computer but could also be a printer, fax machine, cell phone, or PDA. This electronic device may be central to the investigation as it could contain valuable evidence that could help to solve the case. The information contained in the device must be investigated in the proper manner in order to be relied upon in a court of law.

Cyber crime investigation requires extensive research and highly specialized skills, and follows a series of investigation phases and analysis techniques. In the first phase of the investigation, the investigator does a preliminary analysis and gathers all the initial information that he or she can from the scene of the crime. Next, the investigator works on image acquisition and recovery. During this process the investigator extracts the details of all the images and documents recovered from the scene of the crime. Finally, the investigator performs a detailed analysis and prepares a detailed final report to present before the court.

In several cyber crimes, the key evidence is likely to reside on the hardware associated with the computer. However, there are other places from which the evidence can be obtained. Evidence can be found in recorded messages on a telephone, handwritten documents, and organizers. The evidence found isn't always acceptable in a court of law. A skilled and proficient investigator with good experience is needed to search for legally permissible evidence.

Due to the sophistication of the computer industry, certain factors such as collection of clues, attention to the details of the method of attacks and identification of the appropriate evidence are of critical importance. An investigator needs to check the proper documentation of the evidence found and its compliance with the chain of custody. Presenting the evidence in a manner acceptable in a court of law is what determines whether the case is won or lost.

Key Steps in a Forensic Investigation

The following procedure explains the steps involved in a forensic investigation:

1. The investigation is initiated the moment the computer crime is suspected.
2. The immediate response is to collect preliminary evidence. This includes photographing the scene and marking the evidence.
3. A court warrant for seizure (if required) is obtained.
4. First responder procedures are performed.
5. Evidence is seized at the crime scene. After seizure, the evidence is numbered and safely secured.
6. The evidence is securely transported to the forensic laboratory.
7. Two bit-stream copies of the evidence are created. The original disk must not be tampered with as it might change the time stamps.
8. An MD5 checksum is generated on the images.
9. A chain of custody is prepared. Any change to this chain calls into question the admissibility of the evidence.
10. The original evidence is stored in a secure location, preferably away from an easily accessible location.
11. The image copy is analyzed for evidence.
12. A forensic report is prepared. It describes the forensic method and recovery tools used.
13. The report is submitted to the client.
14. If required, the investigator may attend court and testify as an expert witness.

Rules of Forensic Investigations

A forensic examiner must keep in mind certain rules to be applied during a computer forensic examination. The rules of computer forensics must be followed while handling and analyzing the evidence to ensure the integrity of the evidence is safeguarded and accepted in a court of law.

The forensic examiner must make duplicate copies of the original evidence and start by examining only the duplicates. The duplicate copy must be an accurate replication of the original, and the forensic examiner must also authenticate the duplicate copy so queries raised against the integrity of the evidence can be avoided.

Sometimes, changes to the evidence may be inevitable. For example, the memory and/or temporary files on the system may be modified while booting up or shutting down the system. These modifications are natural, and the extent and reason for these modifications must be recorded.

The computer forensic examiner must not continue with the investigation if the examination is going to be beyond his or her knowledge or skill level. In these circumstances, the forensic investigator must either ask for assistance from an experienced specialist investigator or undergo training in that particular field to enhance his or her knowledge or skill base. It would be wise to discontinue the investigation if it is going to cause damage to the case's outcome.

Need for Forensic Investigators

A *forensic investigator*, by virtue of his or her skills and experience, helps organizations and law enforcement agencies investigate and prosecute the perpetrators of cyber crimes. If a technically inexperienced person examines the computer involved in the crime, it will almost certainly result in rendering any evidence found inadmissible in a court of law.

A forensic investigator performs the following tasks:

- Determines the extent of any damage done during the crime
- Recovers data of investigative value from computers involved in crimes
- Gathers evidence in a forensically sound manner
- Ensures that the evidence is not damaged in any way
- Creates an image of the original evidence without tampering with it to maintain the original evidence's integrity
- Guides the officials in carrying out the investigation. At times, it is required that the forensic investigator produce the evidence, describing the procedure involved in its discovery.
- Reconstructs the damaged disks or other storage devices, and uncovers the information hidden on the computer
- Analyzes the evidence data found
- Prepares the analysis report
- Updates the organization about various attack methods and data recovery techniques, and maintains a record of them (following a variant of methods to document) regularly
- Addresses the issue in a court of law and attempts to win the case by testifying in court

Successful computer forensic investigators are well versed in more than one computer platform, including older ones such as MS-DOS and Windows 9x. They are familiar with Linux, Macintosh, and the current Windows platforms. The investigators also develop and maintain contact with computing, networking, and investigating professionals. It also helps for them to keep a log of contacts they have made and record the names of other professionals with whom they have worked. Future forensic investigators can then learn from the information that is provided by these experts.

Accessing Computer Forensic Resources

The Internet has many sites that help computer forensic investigators stay in touch with the growing technical world. Many forensic investigators also use news services that are devoted to computer forensics. Aspiring investigators are encouraged to join various discussion groups and associations to access resources regarding computer forensics. The following two associations offer computer forensic information:

- Computer Technology Investigators Northwest
- High Technology Crime Investigation Association

These user groups can be helpful when information is needed about unknown operating systems encountered during a computer forensic investigation. Outside experts can provide information regarding a case that is still being investigated. These experts can also provide insight into the locations to be searched for incriminating evidence or even help to solve the case itself.

Role of Digital Evidence

When intruders bypass the security settings of a victim's computer or network, they often leave evidence that can serve as clues to document the attack. Certain factors that can contain valuable evidence include:

- Use/abuse of the Internet, indicating the intruder probably exchanged some type of communication or was able to install malware on the victim's computer
- Production of false documents and accounts, which indicates that the intruder is probably concealing something
- Encrypted or password-protected material, which indicates that the intruder is transferring or hiding some secret information
- Abuse of the systems, as when the attacker is using the victim's computer as a zombie or bot to further the attacker's criminal activity
- E-mail contact between suspects/conspirators, which could indicate that more than one intruder is involved and that some sort of collusion has taken place

- Theft of commercial secrets or proprietary information
- Unauthorized transmission of confidential information
- Records of movements within the company, allowing the attacker to benefit from insider knowledge
- Malicious attacks on the computer systems themselves, up to and including denial-of-service attacks
- Stealing names and addresses of the user's or company's contacts

Understanding Corporate Investigations

Private investigations involve private companies and attorneys addressing a company's policy violations and litigation disputes such as wrongful termination. In a corporate investigation, the computer forensic investigator must keep in mind that the business must continue with minimal interference in work during the process of investigation. After the investigation, the company should minimize or eliminate similar litigations. Industrial espionage is the foremost crime in corporate investigations.

Corporate computer crimes usually involve crimes such as e-mail harassment, falsification of information, embezzlement, fraud, and industrial espionage. Any individual with access to a system can commit these crimes.

One of the most common corporate crimes is embezzlement. Corporations are networks of relationships based upon trust. When it is discovered that the clients of a company are being overbilled, the question of embezzlement arises. The task of the computer forensic investigator revolves around reconstructing the electronic trail of when and where the crime was committed.

Another common corporate computer crime is corporate sabotage. Usually a frustrated employee of the firm commits corporate sabotage. This individual may join a rival firm and pass on sensitive company data. In later stages this crime could lead to industrial espionage, which will intensify in the long run. Corporate organizations can prevent these crimes by creating, distributing, and enforcing appropriate policies.

Enterprise Theory of Investigation (ETI)

Though the media frequently focuses on the conviction of the leaders of major criminal enterprises, many lesser-known individuals belonging to the same criminal organizations are also sent to prison. The ETI has become the standard investigative model that the FBI employs in conducting investigations against major criminal organizations. It encourages a proactive attack on the structure of the criminal enterprise rather than viewing each criminal act as an isolated crime.

The *ETI* is a methodology of investigating criminal activity that uses a holistic approach to look at any criminal activity as a piece of a criminal operation rather than as a single criminal act. It has been proved powerful in identifying criminals who have escaped prosecution despite the fact that those criminal organizations ceased to exist.

By combining the ETI with favorable state and federal legislation, law enforcement can target and dismantle entire criminal enterprises in one criminal indictment rather than having to pursue each criminal act one at a time.

The ETI is a variant from the traditional investigative methods and can seem more complex and time consuming. Nevertheless, it has proved to be more effective in prosecuting criminal enterprises.

The value of ETI can be recognized if the underlying motive is identified as financial profit for most criminal enterprises. It analyzes the enterprise's full range of criminal activities, determining which components allow the criminal enterprise to operate and profit from its illegal activities.

The ETI is successful in investigating and prosecuting cases involving criminal organizations with a hierarchal structure of criminal activities. In such cases, the investigation can be initiated from the lower level, where there is maximum chance for identifying the specific criminal activities more easily.

The benefit of applying ETI is that, because of the diversity of the criminal organizations, it discovered new vulnerabilities in the enterprise organizations providing law enforcement agencies with opportunities to identify the more illicit activities.

Legal Issues

It is not always possible for a computer forensic expert to separate the legal issues surrounding the evidence from the practical aspects of computer forensics. The expert should be able to consider all possible conclusions of the investigations in order to be free from bias. The evidence presented should be admissible in a court of law and meet relevant evidence laws. It must be not be tampered with and must be fully accounted for from the time of collection to the time of presentation in court. To present a case in court, all information gathered during the investigation must be properly documented. The laws concerning digital evidence should be strictly adhered to in order to avoid inadmissibility in court.

Forensic experts must do the following:

- Adhere to the chain of custody
- Be thoroughly equipped with the knowledge of law that is applied in that jurisdiction
- Present evidence that is:
  - Authentic
  - Accurate
  - Whole
  - Acceptable
  - Admissible

Experts should test their evidence against the requirements to make sure it can be presented before a court of law. All evidence collection and analysis procedures should also be repeatable, so that in case of any doubt the procedures can be demonstrated in court.

Reporting the Results

Reporting is a major part of any investigative process. All investigation efforts will be in vain if the final report is either incomplete or incomprehensible to target users. Computer forensic experts' reports are also used as evidence during trials in a court of law.

The format and content of an investigation report depends on various factors including: type of case, what information was made available to the investigator, what business processes are affected due to attacks, and the target audience of the report.

A good investigation report contains the following information:

- Methods of investigation
- Adequate supporting data
- Description of data collection techniques
- Calculations used
- Error analysis
- Results and comments
- Graphs and statistics explaining the results
- References
- Appendices
- Acknowledgments
- Litigation support reports

The information should be organized so that anyone can read and understand the report without referring to enclosures or other material.

Chapter Summary

- Computer forensics is the preservation, identification, extraction, interpretation, and documentation of computer evidence, to include the rules of evidence, legal processes, integrity of evidence, factual reporting of the information found, and providing expert opinion in a court of law or other legal and/or administrative proceeding as to what was found.
- The need for computer forensics has increased because computer crimes are increasing.

- The overall objective of all computer forensic phases (preservation, identification, extraction, interpretation, and documentation) is to detect a computer incident, identify the intruder, and prosecute the perpetrator in a court of law.
- IT systems and information security must be used to protect organizations from cyber crime activities.
- Forensic readiness supports an organization's prerequisite need to protect and use digital evidence.
- Cyber crime is any illegal act involving a computer, its systems, or its applications.
- Cyber crime investigations require extensive research, highly specialized skills, and follow a series of investigation phases and analysis techniques.
- A forensic results report may be used as evidence if properly documented and supported by the testimony of a trained forensic investigator.

Review Questions

1. List the various computer forensic flaws and risks.

   _____

   _____

2. Give a few examples of cyber crime.

   _____

   _____

3. How do you maintain professional conduct in a computer forensic investigation?

   _____

   _____

4. Describe the process for a computer forensic investigation.

   _____

   _____

5. Describe the methodologies involved in computer forensics.

   _____

   _____

6. Describe four types of computer crimes.

   _____

   _____

7. What is involved in an internal attack?

   _____

   _____

8. How are cyber crimes categorized?

   _____

   _____

Hands-On Projects

1. Follow these steps:

   ■ Visit the Digital Forensics Research Web site at *http://www.dfrws.org*.

   ■ Read the archives.

   ■ Read the various presentations.

2. Follow these steps:

   ■ Navigate to Chapter 1 of the Student Resource Center.

   ■ Open and read the document titled "computer_crime_study.pdf."

3. Follow these steps:

   ■ Navigate to Chapter 1 of the Student Resource Center.

   ■ Open and read the document titled "legal issues in computer forensics1.pdf."

4. Follow these steps:

   ■ Navigate to Chapter 1 of the Student Resource Center.

   ■ Open and read the document titled "oseles_2.pdf."

Chapter 2

Computer Forensics Lab

Objectives

After completing the chapter, you should be able to:

- Understand and evaluate physical security needs
- Understand evidence lockers and how to secure them
- Create a forensic work area
- Configure a computer forensic lab
- Understand and evaluate equipment needs
- Understand basic forensic workstation requirements
- Understand the tools and software forensic investigators use
- Understand data destruction industry standards

Key Terms

Amperage   a measurement of the amount of electric current

Bandwidth   the width of the range of frequencies that an electronic signal uses on a given transmission medium

Bookrack   a small shelf that is used in a forensic lab to hold reference materials

Business case   the justification to upper management or a lender for purchasing new equipment, software, or other tools when upgrading your facility

Configuration management   the process of keeping track of all changes made to hardware, software, and firmware throughout the life of a system; source code management and revision control are part of this.

Risk management   the decision-making process involving considerations of political, social, economic, and engineering factors with relevant risk assessments relating to a potential hazard so as to develop, analyze, and compare regulatory options and to select the optimal regulatory response for safety from that hazard

Telecommunications Electronics Material Protected from Emanating Spurious Transmissions (TEMPEST)   the external electromagnetic radiation that radiates from any data processing equipment and the various security measures used to prevent that radiation from being captured or monitored

Case Example

Long before computer forensics was seen as a serious profession, the Air Force Computer Forensics Laboratory had cracked a case that involved recreating the evidence from floppy disks that were seemingly beyond repair.

Joseph Snodgrass, who was accused of killing his wife, had destroyed the main evidence, two floppy disks that contained information linked to the crime, by cutting the disks into 23 pieces. The investigators at the Air Force Computer Forensics Laboratory succeeded in rejoining the broken pieces. Evidence on the floppy disks revealed that Mr. Snodgrass had increased his wife's life insurance policy and had hired a hit man to murder her. He was found guilty of the crime. Currently, Joseph Snodgrass is serving a life sentence.

In July 1998, the Air Force Computer Forensics Laboratory became a Defense Department facility under the Defense Reform Initiative.

Introduction to the Computer Forensic Lab

This chapter describes the needs of a forensic investigator, such as the lab and the office. The lab is an important part of any forensic investigation. The chapter discusses the physical security needs of a lab and recommends how to maintain security. It talks about the requirements of a forensic lab and what equipment is needed.

Physical Security Needs of a Forensic Lab

For a forensic lab, security is paramount. The following are some of the physical security considerations of a lab:

- *Access to emergency services*: There should be easy access to emergency services, such as the fire department. Emergency service vehicles must be able to easily access the site and the buildings on the site. The site must also have an area that allows for shipping and receiving without compromising the physical security measures of the lab.

- *Lighting at the site*: The site must have proper lighting designed to augment security and discourage vandalism and unauthorized access to the lab. It should be similar to the campus lighting of a university that conducts night classes.

- *Physical environment of the lab*: The following design features should be avoided:
  - Bushes within 10 feet of the lab premises
  - Clusters of bushes around the premises
  - Tall evergreen trees

- *Structural design of parking*: The parking lot of the lab must be divided into certain levels. These are a few recommendations for designing the levels of parking:
  - *Level 1*: Unsecured level that must be close to the visitor's entrance
  - *Level 2*: Partially secured and fenced-in area used for shipping, biological and toxic waste pickup, and various other activities that require minimum security
  - *Level 3*: Secured place where staff can access the lab at any hour of the day and that can be accessed using only proximity keys or card keys
  - *Level 4*: High-security area that only authorized personnel can access and that security personnel monitor

Physical Security Recommendations for a Forensic Lab

The level of physical security required for a forensic lab depends on the nature of the investigations that are carried out in the lab. The assessment of risk for a forensic lab varies from organization to organization. If an organization is a regional forensic lab, then the risk is high, as the lab most likely deals with multiple cases and different evidences. This may not be true for a forensic lab of a private firm.

Basic Requirements

Basic security needs, such as keeping a log register at the entrance of the lab, should not be overlooked. The log register should contain the following information for each visitor:

- name of the visitor
- date and time of the visit
- purpose of the visit
- name of the official the visitor has come to see
- place the visitor has come from
- address of the visitor

The visitor should be given a visitor's pass so that the visitor can be easily distinguished from the lab staff. To provide an additional layer of protection, an intrusion alarm can be placed in the lab. Guards should be deployed near the premises of the lab. Closed-circuit cameras should be placed in the lab and its premises to monitor human movements within the lab. All of the windows of the lab should be kept closed. This helps prevent unauthorized physical access to the lab through covert channels.

Workstation Security

Workstations should be shielded from transmitting electromagnetic signals. It is a known fact that electronic equipment emits electromagnetic radiation. There are certain pieces of equipment that can intercept this radiation. The radiation can be used to determine the data that the equipment is transmitting or displaying. There is a solution to shield the emissions. The U.S. Department of Defense has named this solution Telecommunications Electronics Material Protected from Emanating Spurious Transmissions, or TEMPEST.

TEMPEST

The National Industrial Security Program Operating Manual (NISPOM) states, "*TEMPEST* is an unclassified short name referring to investigations and studies of compromising emanations. Compromising emanations are unintentional intelligence-bearing signals that, if intercepted and analyzed, will disclose classified information when it is transmitted, received, handled, or otherwise processed by any information processing equipment (U.S. Department of Defense, 2006, p. 11-1-1)."

To prevent eavesdropping, TEMPEST labs can be constructed. Sheets of metal that are good conductors, such as copper, should be used for lining the walls, ceilings, and floors. Even the power cables need to be insulated to prevent radiation. Also, the telephones within the lab must have line filters.

It is costly to build a TEMPEST lab, as checks and maintenance have to be carried out at regular intervals. As a replacement for a TEMPEST lab, some vendors have come up with workstations that emit only low amounts of radiation. The cost of this kind of workstation is higher than a typical forensic workstation.

Fire Safety

Fire can be disastrous in a forensic lab. Any electrical device can be a source of fire, though this does not generally happen with computers. On a few occasions, short circuits can also damage cables. These short circuits might even ignite flammable items close by.

Fires may break out in computers if the servo-voice coil actuators in a hard drive freeze due to damage in the drive. If the actuators freeze, the head assembly stops moving. The internal programming of the disk tries to force the head assembly to move by applying more power to the servo-voice coil actuators. The components of the drive can handle a certain amount of power before they fail and overload the ribbon cable connecting the drive to the motherboard. These ribbon cables do not respond well to excessive power. High voltage passed through a ribbon cable causes sparks to fly.

Fire-Suppression Systems

The following are some fire-suppression systems that should be in place in a forensic lab:

- Dry chemical fire extinguisher system to deal with fires that occur due to chemical reactions
- Sprinkler system that should be checked frequently to make sure it is still working

Fire extinguishers should be placed within and outside the lab. Before the fire extinguishers are in place, the lab personnel and the guards should be given instructions on how to use them so that in case of a fire the trained staff will know how to use the equipment effectively.

Evidence Locker Recommendations

The containers used to store evidence must be secured so that unauthorized persons cannot access the evidence. They should be located in a restricted area that is only accessible to lab personnel. All evidence containers must be monitored, and they must be locked when not in use.

The storage containers or cabinets should be made of steel and should include either an internal cabinet lock or an external padlock. There must be a limited number of duplicate keys so that authorized access is limited. Evidence can also be stored in safes of superior quality to secure the evidence from fire damage. Media devices and digital media should be stored in media safes.

Lab personnel must regularly inspect the content of the evidence storage containers to ensure that only current evidence is stored. Evidence from closed cases must be moved to other containers.

Checking the Security of a Forensic Lab

Lab personnel should periodically check the security of a forensic lab to ensure that the security policy is being followed. The following are the steps that must be followed to check for security policy compliance:

- Examine the ceiling, floor, and exterior walls of the lab at least once a month to check for structural integrity.
- Examine the doors to ensure they close and lock correctly.
- Check if the locks are working properly or if they need to be replaced.
- Examine the log register to make sure all entries are correct and complete.
- Check the log sheets for evidence containers to check when the containers were opened and when they were closed.
- Acquire evidence that is not being processed and store it in a secure place.

Work Area of a Computer Forensic Lab

The forensic lab should be built in an area where human traffic is light. An ideal lab consists of two forensic workstations and one ordinary workstation with Internet connectivity. The number of forensic workstations varies according to the number of cases and processes handled in the lab.

Work Area Configuration

The configuration of the work area depends on the budget that is allocated for the forensic lab. On average, the workstation occupies the area of a desk. This is assuming that the cases and analyses the lab handles are not heavy. However, as the complexity and number of cases increase, the workstation area increases. It is advised to have separate rooms for supervisors and cubicles for investigators.

The work area should have ample space so that there is also a space for case discussions among investigators. There should be enough space for each workstation so that the investigator is not forced to work surrounded by stacks of files and equipment. If this were the case, the productivity of the investigator would decrease, thus hampering the investigative process. The layout of the forensic lab should be well planned and should be scalable so that there is room for expansion.

General Configuration of a Forensic Lab

A forensic lab should have the following:

- *Workstations*: A forensic lab should have both forensic and nonforensic workstations for investigative purposes. There should be ample space in which to disassemble a workstation if the need arises during the investigative process.
- *UPS*: Power failure during an investigative process can be costly for an investigator. The need for an uninterruptible power supply (UPS) arises as a preventive measure. Separate backup power generators are recommended for a forensic lab. Any electrical connections should be monitored, as any fluctuations in voltage may also disrupt the power supply or damage electrical equipment.

- *Bookracks*: **Bookracks** in a forensic lab are necessary to hold all the reference books, articles, and magazines that an investigator would need in the course of an investigation. This helps clear clutter off the desks, giving more space to the investigators.

- *Necessary software*: Licensed versions of all the software required for computer forensic investigation should be readily available to an investigator at any time during the investigation. Demo versions of forensic software are not recommended, as most demo versions have limited functionality. Having licensed versions also helps investigators during court trials. However, as long as the demo version of a tool is fully functional, an investigator can reliably use the tool.

- *Reference materials*: During the course of an investigation, investigators may need to consult reference materials in order to solve a particular problem or follow a particular process.

- *Safe locker and storage shelf*: A safe locker large enough to store equipment required for forensic investigations should be available in the lab. This helps an investigator categorize the equipment stored in the rack so that he or she can easily locate the kind of equipment needed during an investigation. Safe lockers also help keep the equipment free from wear and tear, and away from dust and other foreign particles that may hamper the equipment's performance. A storage shelf is used to stock equipment that is not in use.

- *LAN and Internet connectivity*: To share information among forensic workstations or to perform certain tasks, a LAN is required. LAN connectivity and Internet connectivity are required to do forensic investigation of remote networks.

Equipment Required in a Forensic Lab

What equipment is needed in a forensic lab depends on the nature of the forensic investigations carried out in the lab. Some of the pieces of equipment common to any computer forensic lab are:

- *Cabinets*: Each cabinet should contain a computer system that has a CPU with high processing capacity, high-speed RAM, drive bays for a CD drive with read/write capabilities, hard disks, tape drives, and floppy drives.

- *Printers and scanners*: Printers are necessary for printing investigation reports or any materials that can be used as references during investigations. Scanners allow investigators to recreate original documents from damaged documents obtained from the scene of a crime and to check for faint evidence.

- *Additional hard drives*: Additional hard drives should be available for investigators in case they need to make backup copies of hard drives that contain data relevant to an investigation.

- *Tape drives*: Tape drives should be compatible with the media formats that an investigator is likely to come across during an investigation.

Electrical Needs

The following elements should be kept in mind when considering the electrical needs of a computer forensic lab:

- *Amperage*: The lab must be provided with the amperage required to power all of the electrical equipment in the lab. **Amperage** is a measurement of the electric current.

- *Emergency power and lighting*: Emergency power and lighting should be provided for the following parts of the lab:
  - All the evidence sections
  - All the security sections, electronic security systems, and telephones
  - X-ray processing rooms and photography dark rooms

- *Electrical outlets*: There must be easy access to the electrical outlets in the lab.

- *UPS*: All the workstations and electrical equipment—including laboratory instrumentation, the automated fingerprint identification system (AFIS), combined DNA identification systems, integrated ballistic imaging systems, and LABNET—require a UPS. A centralized UPS is preferred.

Communications

The following factors should be considered when assessing the communications systems available in the lab:

- *Bandwidth*: *Bandwidth* refers to the width of the range of frequencies that an electronic signal uses on a given transmission medium. There should be a dedicated broadband connection for network and voice communications.
- *Dial-up access*: Dial-up Internet access must be available for workstations in the laboratory.
- *Disconnection*: Forensic computers must be disconnected from the network when they are not being used.
- *Network*: A dedicated network is preferred for the forensic computers, as they require continuous access to the Internet and other resources on the network when in use.

Basic Workstation Requirements in a Forensic Lab

Forensics workstations are high-end computers with fast processing speeds and large amounts of memory and disk storage. These workstations are used for critical processes such as duplicating data, recovering data from deleted files, analyzing data over the network, and retrieving data from the slack. These workstations are loaded with forensic tools that help an investigator during an investigation. Many high-end and low-end processes are carried out during a particular investigation. Thus, the hardware configuration of a forensic workstation, which is used for high-end processing, is different from that of a workstation used for doing routine tasks. The hardware requirements for a basic forensic workstation are as follows:

- Processor with high computing speed
- 256 MB RAM for satisfying minimum processing requirements
- DVD-ROM with read/write capabilities
- Motherboard that supports IDE, SCSI, and USB, with a slot for a LAN/WAN card and a fan attached for cooling the processor
- Tape drive, USB drive, and removable drive bays
- Monitor, keyboard, and mouse
- Minimum of two hard drives for loading two different operating systems, preferably Windows XP and Linux

Recommended Hardware Peripherals

The following are the hardware peripherals that must be kept in stock at all times to ensure that an investigator always has the necessary tools:

- 40-pin 18-inch and 36-inch IDE cables, both ATA-33 and ATA-100 or faster
- SATA cables
- A variety of detachable storage media like Jaz cartridges, Zip cartridges, and USB drives
- Other electronic storage devices (CompactFlash cards, SmartMedia cards, Secure Digital cards, Multi-Media cards, and Memory Stick)
- CD/DVD readers and writers
- Ribbon cables for floppy disks
- Extra IDE hard drives
- Extra RAM
- Extra SCSI cards
- Graphics cards (ISA, PCI, AGP, and PCI Express)
- Extra power cords
- A variety of hard disk drives
- Laptop hard drive connectors

- Handheld devices
- Supplementary storage devices for creating bit-stream copies or clones of the suspect storage media for examination purposes

Maintaining Operating System and Application Inventories

Forensic investigators use a variety of software applications. These pieces of software must be updated regularly to ensure that the investigators are using the most recent versions. Operating systems must also be updated regularly to ensure that the latest patches have been applied. The following are the applications and operating systems that must be maintained:

- Windows Vista, XP, 2003, and 2000 operating systems
- Linux, Unix, and Mac OS X operating systems
- Microsoft Office XP, 2007, 2003, 2000, 97, and 95
- Quicken
- Programming language applications such as Visual Studio
- Specialized viewers such as QuickView and ACDSee
- Corel Office Suite
- StarOffice/OpenOffice
- Peachtree accounting applications
- Older operating systems and applications such as MS-DOS, Windows 3.11, and Novell for examining older systems
- Forensic software with advanced features and functionalities, such as:
  - Bit-stream backup utilities
  - Password recovery tools
  - Recovery tools for deleted data
  - Partition recovery tools
  - Searching tools
  - Firewalls and intrusion detection systems
  - Updated antivirus software

Common Terms

- *Configuration management*: The process of keeping track of all changes made to hardware, software, and firmware throughout the life of a system; source code management and revision control are part of this
- *Risk management*: The decision-making process involving considerations of political, social, economic, and engineering factors with relevant risk assessments relating to a potential hazard so as to develop, analyze, and compare regulatory options and to select the optimal regulatory response for safety from that hazard
- *Business case*: The justification to upper management or a lender for purchasing new equipment, software, or other tools when upgrading your facility

Required Forensic Tools

Forensic professionals use a variety of tools both in the lab and in the field. The following sections discuss the various types of tools they use and the purpose of each type.

Storage Bags

When evidence is collected in the field, the forensic investigator needs to store the evidence for transport back to the lab so it can be examined. The investigator must make sure that the evidence is not damaged or tampered with, so different types of bags have been developed to make sure evidence stays safe and secure. The following describes some of the different types of storage bags:

- *Wireless storage bags*: These types of bags are used to store wireless devices. The fabric used to make these bags shields the wireless devices from wireless signals that could potentially alter or eliminate data on the devices. Figure 2-1 shows Paraben's version, called the Wireless StrongHold Bag. There are also tents that provide the same capabilities. An investigator with a laptop sits inside the tent while he or she captures the data from a wireless device. The data is still protected, but the investigator doesn't have to wait to get back to the lab to acquire it. Figure 2-2 shows Paraben's Wireless StrongHold Tent.

- *Passport bags*: Many passports contain radio-frequency identification (RFID) chips. These types of bags shield these chips so that data cannot be read from them. As more and more passports are fitted with RFID chips, securing the data stored on them is becoming more and more vital. Figure 2-3 shows Paraben's Passport StrongHold Bag.

Remote Chargers

Remote chargers are used to provide power for devices that may contain vital evidence. The chargers allow investigators to retrieve evidence from devices such as phones and other handhelds that have run out of power. Remote chargers typically are equipped with tips that fit into a variety of devices made by different manufacturers. Figure 2-4 shows Paraben's version of a remote charger.

Write Block Protection Devices

These tools prevent the alteration or erasure of data during an investigation. Typically, these devices are used when examining or copying data from a storage device to a forensic laptop or workstation. They can be used for a variety of devices, from hard drives to USB drives to media cards. There are different types for different storage device connections. For instance, an SATA write block protection device (Figure 2-5) allows an investigator

Figure 2-1 Paraben's Wireless StrongHold Bag is used to shield wireless devices from outside signals.

Figure 2-2 Paraben's Wireless StrongHold Tent allows a forensic investigator to securely pull data from a wireless device.

Figure 2-3   Paraben's Passport StrongHold Bag is used to keep data stored on RFID chips in passports secure.

Figure 2-4   Remote chargers allow a forensic investigator to provide power to any device in the field.

Figure 2-5   This write block protection device allows an investigator to attach a storage device to a computer's SATA connector.

Figure 2-6   This device allows an investigator to attach a storage device to a computer's USB or Firewire port without fear of altering the data.

to attach a storage device to a computer's SATA connector, and a USB or Firewire write block protection device (Figure 2-6) allows an investigator to attach a storage device to a computer's USB or Firewire port.

Data Acquisition Tools

- *Cables*: The forensic professional should have all the cables he or she will need to connect a laptop to a device that may contain evidence. Different kinds of devices use different kinds of cables. Often, a forensic investigator will carry a bag that contains all of the cables he or she may need in the field. Figure 2-7 shows a USB to DB9 cable for connecting serial devices to a computer's USB port.

- *Rapid action imaging devices (RAIDs)*: These devices allow a forensic investigator to copy a suspect hard drive to a clean hard drive very quickly. Then the investigator can examine and analyze the copy without disturbing the original data. Figure 2-8 shows a RAID.

- *SIM card readers*: The devices are used to extract data from the SIM cards used in cell phones and other devices. As in the example in Figure 2-9, SIM card readers typically allow an investigator to connect a

Figure 2-7 This cable connects a serial device to a computer's USB port.

Figure 2-9 This SIM card reader connects a SIM card to a computer's USB port.

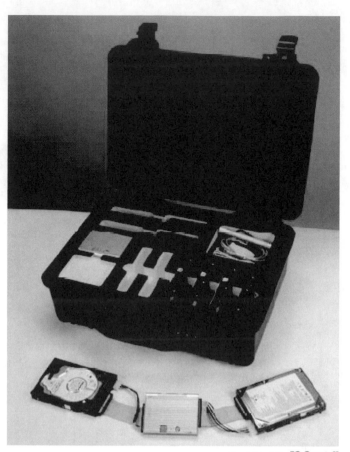

Figure 2-8 This RAID is used to quickly make copies of hard drives.

SIM card to a computer's USB port. The investigator then uses software to examine and extract the data on the card.

- *Video-capture devices*: Sometimes, there may be no way to get data off of a device, either because the device's connection point is broken or because the investigator doesn't have the proper hardware. In these cases, the investigator can use a device that holds the suspect device still and takes video of the screen. Using an imaging device allows an investigator to scroll through all of the data on the device and capture video only of the screens that contain important data. This video can be shown on a mobile forensic laptop, displayed with a projector, or streamed over the Internet. Figure 2-10 shows Paraben's Project-a-Phone.

Forensic Archive and Restore Devices

Investigators use forensic archive and restore robotic devices to archive forensic data. These devices can copy a large number of CD-ROM or DVD media discs containing forensic data. Many of these devices can also print labels for the copies so the investigator will know what is on the discs.

Mobile Forensic Laptops

Mobile forensic laptops are equipped with all the specialized software a forensic specialist needs in the field. They have fast processors, large amounts of RAM, and large hard drives. They are equipped with DVD burners and media card readers. They also have some form of write block protection, provided either through hardware or software. Figure 2-11 shows a forensic laptop and some of its related peripherals.

Forensic Workstations

Like forensic laptops, forensic workstations have all the software a forensic specialist needs. They also are equipped with DVD burners and media card readers, and they are typically top-of-the-line systems. Forensic

Figure 2-10   This device is used to record video of a device's screens when there is no other way to acquire the data on the device.

Figure 2-11   A typical mobile forensic laptop has all the software and connections a forensic investigator needs to acquire and analyze data in the field.

Figure 2-12 This is the
kind of workstation
found in a forensic lab.

workstations also allow for the hot swapping of hard drives. Using this functionality, investigators can connect a suspect hard drive to a workstation for analysis without having to turn off the workstation. Write block protection is also provided. Figure 2-12 shows a forensic workstation.

Imaging Workstations

Forensic laboratories are equipped with workstations devoted solely to imaging storage devices, including hard drives, CDs, DVDs, USB drives, and media cards. These workstations typically store the images on tapes. Some of these workstations include password-cracking capabilities so data can be accessed even on password-protected storage devices.

Software

Forensic professionals use a variety of software tools for different tasks. Most of this software is used for extracting and analyzing data on storage devices, but there is also software for examining a live computer. These tools can both examine and record the live system state, including the registry, the running processes, the logged-in users, the files on all connected drives, and the network configuration.

Investigations at a Computer Forensic Lab

The following are some of the types of computer forensic investigations that are conducted at a computer forensic laboratory:

- Child pornography and sexual exploitation
- Use of e-mail, instant messaging, and chat
- Computer hacking and network intrusion
- Copyright infringement
- Software piracy
- Intellectual property disputes
- Identity theft
- Online auction fraud

Data Destruction Industry Standards

- American: DoD 5220.22-M
- American: NAVSO P-5239-26 (RLL)
- American: NAVSO P-5239-26 (MFM)
- German: VSITR
- Russian: Russian Standard, GOST P50739-95

- Credit card fraud
- Other financial frauds and schemes
- Telecommunications fraud
- Threats, harassment, and/or stalking
- Extortion and/or blackmail
- Online gambling
- Drug abuse and/or distribution
- Employee or employer misconduct
- Theft, robbery, and/or burglary

Procedures at a Computer Forensic Lab

Various procedures are performed at a computer forensic lab. The following is a list of typical procedures:

- Creating an exact replica of a hard disk drive or other storage device so the evidence can be evaluated and processed from a forensic evidence file, guaranteeing that the best-suited evidence is preserved
- Identifying leads and computer evidence contained in files and slack space, which can determine the outcome of a case
- Documenting findings and providing expert witness testimony to help clarify technical computer issues during the litigation process
- Finding data—such as deleted e-mail and intentionally altered data—on a formatted or purposely damaged hard drive, documenting and analyzing the data, and recording the information in reports that are then presented to the client and/or in litigation

All procedures in a computer forensic lab must meet federal standards, including security, confidentiality, and data destruction standards.

Chapter Summary

- An ideal lab consists of two forensic workstations and one ordinary workstation with Internet connectivity.
- A lab should be inspected on a regular basis to check if the policies and procedures implemented are followed.
- A forensic lab should be under surveillance at all times to protect it from intrusions.
- Forensic investigators use a wide variety of software and hardware tools in the field and in the lab.

Review Questions

1. What is the purpose of a write block protection device?

   _____

   _____

2. What is a TEMPEST lab? Why would anyone choose not to build a TEMPEST lab?

   _____

   _____

3. Write down the various types of computer forensic investigations that can be conducted at a computer forensic lab.

   _____

   _____

4. What is the purpose of a log register?

   _____

   _____

5. How can a fire start inside a computer system?

   _____

   _____

6. What is a UPS, and why does a lab need one?

   _____

   _____

7. Describe the recommended features of evidence lockers.

   _____

   _____

8. Identify and describe two types of forensic storage bags.

   _____

   _____

9. Identify and describe the types of software that should be on a mobile forensic laptop.

   _____

   _____

10. Explain the function of forensic archive and restore robotic devices.

   _____

   _____

Hands-On Projects

1. Consider a scenario in which you are designing a computer forensic lab. Decide what equipment you will put in your lab. Compare and contrast this list with the list of equipment described in this chapter.

2. Consider a scenario in which you are establishing the security policy for a computer forensic lab. Making sure to keep in mind all aspects of security, write out your security policy and compare and contrast it with the security recommendations described in this chapter.

3. Perform the following steps:

   ■ Navigate to Chapter 2 of the Student Resource Center.

   ■ Read the document titled "Setting up forensics lab.pdf."

References

U.S. Department of Defense. (2006). *National industrial security program operating manual.* Retrieved from http://fas.org/sgp/library/nispom.htm

Computer Investigation Process

Objectives

After completing this chapter, you should be able to:

- Investigate computer crime
- Develop policies and procedures
- Investigate a company policy violation
- Understand the methodology of investigation
- Evaluate a case (perform case assessment)
- Develop and follow an investigation plan
- Obtain a search warrant
- Understand warning banners
- Collect evidence
- Implement an investigation
- Image an evidence disk
- Examine digital evidence
- Close a case
- Evaluate a case

Key Terms

Best practices   an empirically proven set of methods for performing a task in the best and most efficient way

Bit-stream copy   a bit-by-bit copy of the original storage medium

Chain of custody   a method for documenting the history and possession of a sample from the time of collection, through analysis and data reporting, to its final disposition

DriveSpy   a disk-forensic DOS tool that is designed to emulate and extend the capabilities of DOS to meet forensic needs; it creates direct disk-to-disk forensic duplicates, can copy a range of sectors within or between drives, and can process duplicate drives

File slack the space that exists between the end of a file and the end of the last cluster of the file; see also *slack space*

Host-protected area (HPA) an area of the drive where a certain portion of the drive's contents is hidden from the operating system and file system

Incident an event or series of events that threatens the security of computing systems and networks in an organization

Internet service provider (ISP) a company that provides individuals and other companies access to the Internet and other related services, such as Web site building and virtual hosting

Search warrant a written order issued by a judge that directs a law enforcement officer to search a specific area for a particular piece of evidence

Slack space the space that exists between the end of a file and the end of the last cluster of the file; see also *file slack*

Steganography the art and science of hiding information by embedding messages in other, seemingly harmless messages

Warning banner a message that a user is shown either prior to signing on to a system or immediately thereafter in which the user's responsibilities are detailed and warning messages about monitoring activities are relayed

Case Example

Credentials International is an employment verification agency located in Chicago that assists companies around the globe in hiring the right talent. Sebastian was working as a verification assistant with the firm. He handled clients located in North America.

Credentials International was accused by one of its clients of not validating the credentials of 10 employees who were posted in the firm. The employer, Right4Source, a North American software firm, had hired people for the position of J2EE Developer. Right4Source's HR department found that the employees had faked their experience and certificates for the job.

Initial investigations showed Sebastian's involvement in the scandal.

The investigative team hired by Right4Source sprang into action. The employees of Right4Source caught with fake credentials were cross-questioned. Further investigation revealed a link that each fraudster had in common—Sebastian. A search warrant against Sebastian was issued by the district court.

The senior management of Credentials International was made aware of the search warrant by the investigators. A computer forensics expert was part of the investigative team.

The investigators seized Sebastian's mobile phone and laptop. They also obtained the call record from Sebastian's mobile service provider. The record showed numbers that belonged to the employees of Right4Source who were caught for fraud. Sebastian had made multiple calls to each of them. The team also checked Sebastian's laptop for evidence. The computer forensic investigator made an image of the hard disk of the laptop. Further investigation revealed e-mail conversations with the employees as well as other original documents concerning the employees. The e-mail investigation revealed that Sebastian had committed the fraud for a fee of $2000 per employee.

Sebastian was arrested and taken to the district police department. The law enforcement agents interrogated Sebastian based on the investigative findings. After a series of interrogations, Sebastian confessed to the crime. He was fired from his job, and he was fined $10,000 for committing fraud.

Introduction to Computer Investigation

This chapter introduces the concept of computer investigation and shows the steps involved in investigating computer crime. The first section discusses the importance of determining if an incident has occurred. Following sections discuss how to search for and collect evidence that can be used in a legal case or for a corporate inquiry, how to examine and analyze this evidence, and other matters related to forensic cases.

Investigating Computer Crime

Before starting an investigation, an investigator needs to first determine that an incident has occurred and then assess its impact. An *incident* is an event that threatens the security of a computer system or network in an organization. An investigator must verify any complaints related to an intrusion, as some may turn out to be hoax calls. An intrusion detection system alert may only indicate an attempted, unsuccessful intrusion, or it might be a false alarm. Therefore, an investigator must weigh the strengths, weaknesses, and other known nuances related to the sources and include human factors as well as digital factors.

Policy and Procedure Development

Developing policies and procedures is an important phase in creating a computer forensic unit. The following are the types of policies and procedures that need to be established:

- *A mission statement*: Incorporates the core functions of the unit, which includes high-technology crime investigations, evidence collection, and forensic analysis
- *The personnel requirements for the computer forensic unit*: Includes job descriptions, minimum qualifications, hours of operation, on-call duty status, command structure, and team configuration
- *Administrative considerations*: Includes the following considerations:
  - *Software licensing*: Makes sure that the software tools the unit uses are properly licensed
  - *Resource commitment*: Includes resources such as equipment used by the examiners, ongoing professional development, and software and hardware requirements
  - *Training*: Produces skilled and competent examiners
- *Submission and retrieval of computer forensic service requests*: Develops the guidelines to set up the process for the submission of computer forensic services requests and the acceptance of these requests for the examination of digital evidence
- *Implementation of case-management procedures*: Includes the nature of the crime, court dates, deadlines, possible victims, lawful considerations, and the volatile nature of the evidence
- *Handling of evidence*: Gives the guidelines for receiving, processing, documenting, and preserving the evidence at the time of examination
- *Development of case-processing procedures*: Helps in preserving and processing digital evidence
- *Development of technical procedures*: The following must be documented at the time of the development and validation of procedures:
  - Identifying the task or problem
  - Proposing possible solutions
  - Testing each solution on a known control sample
  - Evaluating the results of the test
  - Finalizing the procedure

Investigating a Company Policy Violation

Every company has a predefined set of policies that each employee has to follow regarding the use of computer equipment owned by the company. Properly drafted company policies regarding the use of electronic media can eliminate the chance of an employee compromising privacy during information retrieval.

Implementing and Enforcing Company Policy

To effectively implement such policies, the company needs to inform each employee of the company policy. Employees who use company resources such as Internet or computer systems for personal use not only violate company policies but also waste resources, time, and money. To take care of company policy violations, forensic examiners or investigators are called in to perform internal investigations. As a computer forensic professional, an investigator has to gather the evidence from the suspect's computer and determine whether a crime or violation of the company policy has occurred. An investigator should follow a standard methodology for investigating company policy violations.

The motive behind company policy violation investigation is not always to take punitive steps. Sometimes, employees just need to be educated, as they might not be aware of the fact that they are violating company policy. If the problem persists, however, the company can take strict action against those employees who continue to violate company policy.

Policy Violation Case Example

Mike is suspected of conducting his own business using a company computer.

- *Situation*: Employee abuse case
- *Nature of the case*: Side business
- *Specifics about the case*: The employee is reportedly conducting a side business on his computer.
- *Type of evidence*: Floppy disk
- *OS*: Windows 2000
- *Known disk format*: FAT32
- *Location of evidence*: The disk that a manager found near Mike's computer; the manager had received complaints from Mike's co-workers that he was spending too much time on his own business and not performing his assigned work duties.

Based on case details, you can determine the case requirements:

- *Type of evidence*: Mike was conducting his own business using his employer's computer.
- *Computer forensics tools*: Tools for duplicating the floppy disk and finding deleted and hidden files
- *Special operating systems*: Any operating systems that had been installed on company computers by the suspect

Mike is only *suspected* of violating company policy; the evidence you obtain might either prove him guilty or help prove his innocence.
Maintain an unbiased perspective, and be objective.

Before Starting the Investigation

A preliminary requirement for an investigation is that a skilled technician is on the team. The technician should be capable enough to analyze and acquire a variety of evidence. The second foremost requirement is a workstation or data recovery lab. The lab should be equipped with the right equipment and forensic tools required for the investigation.

Legal Considerations

One important thing an investigator needs to keep in mind while dealing with cases involving computer crime is to have synchronization with the local district attorney. In some cases, the local district attorney asks for more documentation concerning the chain of evidence after a case is prepared and is ready for trial. In these situations, it can become very difficult to recreate the chain. Therefore, to avoid these situations, an investigator should be aware of what the local district attorney wants and act accordingly.

Some important legal points an investigator should keep in mind are:

- Ensuring the scope of the search
- Checking for possible issues related to the federal statutes applicable (such as the Electronic Communications Privacy Act of 1986 [ECPA] and the Cable Communications Policy Act [CCPA], both as amended by the USA PATRIOT Act of 2001, and the Privacy Protection Act of 1980 [PPA]), state statutes, and local policies and laws

Investigators should contact the legal authorities in cases where the search cannot be limited.

Investigating Methodology

Another underlying component of an investigation is methodology development. Methodology is nothing more than a set of guidelines that is used to maintain consistency.

It can be very difficult to develop a methodology for computer investigations because there are many variables in forensic cases. But there are two things that can give foundation to foolproof analysis and case building: defining the methodology and working accordingly. By defining the methodology, the investigator can have an overview of how forensic cases should be handled in general, even though each case is handled differently.

10 Steps to Prepare for a Computer Forensic Investigation

1. Do not turn the computer off or on, run any programs, or attempt to access data on the computer. An expert will have the appropriate tools and experience to prevent data overwriting, damage from static electricity, or other concerns.

2. Secure any relevant media—including hard drives, laptops, BlackBerrys, PDAs, cell phones, CD-ROMs, DVDs, USB drives, and MP3 players—the subject may have used.

3. Suspend automated document destruction and recycling policies that may pertain to any relevant media or users at the time of the issue.

4. Identify the type of data you are seeking, the information you are looking for, and the urgency level of the examination.

5. Once the machine is secured, obtain information about the machine, the peripherals, and the network to which it is connected.

6. If possible, obtain passwords to access encrypted or password-protected files.

7. Compile a list of names, e-mail addresses, and other identifying information about those with whom the subject might have communicated.

8. If the computer is accessed before the forensic expert is able to secure a mirror image, note the user(s) who accessed it, what files they accessed, and when the access occurred. If possible, find out why the computer was accessed.

9. Maintain a chain of custody for each piece of original media, indicating where the media has been, whose possession it has been in, and the reason for that possession.

10. Create a list of key words or phrases to use when searching for relevant data.

The methodology can also be used as a point of reference, and the investigator can work according to the steps indicated.

An investigator follows standard steps when preparing a forensic case. Most of the steps remain the same for solving any kind of forensic case. These steps are:

1. *Initially assess the case*: The investigator should ask related questions and document people's responses. Company security professionals can relate questions to the seizure of computer equipment and components. Investigators should check for the role of the computer in question and for evidence related to the case.

2. *Determine a preliminary design or approach to the case*: During this step, the investigator prepares a general outline for investigating the case. In the case of an employee violation of company policy, this phase deals with determining whether the employee's computer can be seized during working hours or whether an investigator has to wait until after office hours or the weekend.

3. *Prepare a detailed design*: The investigator refines the general outline that was prepared during the previous step. The investigator plans detailed steps, taking into account the estimated time, resources, and money required to complete each step. This helps the forensic professional track the progress of an investigation and ensures that appropriate controls are in place in case there is deviation from the plan.

4. *Determine what resources are required*: The kind of software used for investigation varies with the OS used by the suspect.

5. *Obtain an evidence disk drive*: The investigator seizes the different kinds of equipment used by any suspects in the case.

6. *Copy an evidence disk drive*: The investigator images the evidence obtained during the previous step onto a different disk and then prepares a forensic copy of the disk.

7. *Identify the risks involved*: An investigator can face a lot of problems while handling a case, so investigators are required to document any problems they expect or constraints they think may occur during the investigation. This documentation of problems is called standard risk assessment. For example, a suspect might have set a logon scheme that shuts down the computer or erases the hard disk if someone wants to change the password.

8. *Minimize the risks*: A forensic professional should look for different ways to minimize the risks identified during the previous step. For example, if the suspect had password-protected the hard drive, the investigator should make multiple copies of the media before starting the investigation. This step will help the investigator achieve the goal of retrieving the information.

9. *Test the design*: The investigator needs to review the decisions made and the steps taken so far. During the review, the investigator can determine whether the steps that have been taken are correct and can be justified.

10. *Analyze and recover the digital evidence*: The investigator can analyze and recover the digital evidence using the software tools and other resources that were determined in the previous steps.

11. *Investigate the recovered data*: Once the data is recovered and analyzed, the investigator can view and organize the data to help prove the guilt or innocence of the suspect.

12. *Complete the case report*: The investigator prepares a complete report containing information about what he or she did and found.

13. *Critique the case*: This step deals with a self-evaluation by the investigator. After the investigation related to the case is completed and the report is prepared, the investigator should review the case to identify successful decisions and actions, and work upon any shortcomings. This will help the investigator deal with future cases.

Evaluating the Case

There are several steps that have to be taken when assessing a case:

1. Initially examine the investigator's service request.

2. Find the legal authority for the forensic examination request.

3. Ensure that the request for assistance is assigned.

4. Provide the complete chain of custody.

5. Check if forensic processes such as analysis of DNA, fingerprints, tool marks, traces, and questioned documents need to be performed on the evidence.

6. Check if there is the possibility to follow investigative methods such as sending a preservation order to an Internet service provider, identifying remote storage locations, and obtaining e-mail. An *Internet service provider (ISP)* is a company that provides Internet access to an individual or organization.

7. Identify the relevance of various peripheral components, such as credit cards, check paper, scanners, and cameras, to the crime scene.

8. Establish the potential evidence being sought.

9. Obtain additional details such as e-mail addresses, the ISP used, and user names.

10. Evaluate the skill levels of the users to identify their expertise in destroying or concealing the evidence.

11. Set the order of evidence examination.

12. Identify whether additional personnel is required.

13. Identify whether additional equipment is required.

Warning Banners

A ***warning banner*** is text that a user usually reads before signing on to a system in which the user's responsibilities while using the system are stated. By proceeding, the user accepts the responsibility of using the computer system and its resources, data, and network access capabilities. The user is required to acknowledge some form of compliance prior to accessing the system's resources. If the system or the application does not have any kind of pre-login capabilities, the banner should be immediately displayed following authorization. If that is not possible, then a printed banner must be placed in common areas where users may access the system and its environments. The banner should warn authorized and unauthorized users about improper use of the system. If any organization wants to monitor a user's activity on state-owned systems, the user must be warned prior to monitoring. Figure 3-1 shows an example of a warning banner.

COMPUTER USAGE WARNING

This computer system is connected to the State of <u>New York</u> computer network, and therefore shall be governed by all local and state policies and laws concerning use of this system and available resources. This computer system, including all related equipment, networks and network devices (specifically including internet access), are provided only for authorized users. <u>Xsecurity School District</u> computer systems may be monitored for all lawful purposes, including to ensure that their use is authorized, for management of the system, to facilitate protection against unauthorized access, and to verify security procedures, survivability and operational security. Monitoring includes active attacks by authorized Xsecurity School District and State of <u>Arkansas Information Technology</u> administrators to test or verify the security of this system. During monitoring, information may be examined, recorded, copied and used for authorized purposes. All information, including personal information, placed on or sent over this system may be monitored. Use of the <u>Xsecurity School District</u> computer system, authorized or unauthorized, constitutes consent to monitoring of this system. Unauthorized use may subject you to criminal prosecution. Evidence of unauthorized use collected during monitoring may be used for administrative, criminal or advesc action. Authorized or unauthorized users of the <u>Xsecurity School District</u> computer system shall have no expectation of privacy while using this system. If criminal activity is discovered, the information will be provided to the appropriate law enforcement officials. Suspected access violations or rule infractions should be reported to the Information Technology Director or the Network Administrator. The Information Technology Director and Network Administrator can be reached at XXXXXXX or XXXXXXX. **Use of this system constitutes consent to monitoring for these purposes and is also an acceptance of the Xsecurity School District Computer Usage Contract which can be found in the student handbook and/or personnel policies as well as by visiting XXXXXXX and clicking on Board Policies.**

Figure 3-1   This is an example of a warning banner that a user sees when signing on to a system.

Purpose of Warning Banners

Warning banners inform users that the system may be monitored to detect improper use and other illicit activity during the time he or she is on the system. This means that the user has no expectation of privacy while he or she is using the system. The presence of these banners

(continues)

eliminates users' claims of ignorance of their responsibilities. Employees must be clearly warned of the penalties for noncompliance with the company's policies. Information handled by computer systems must be adequately protected against unauthorized modification, disclosure, or destruction.

Warning Banners as Part of a Forensic Case

Warnings are a positive step toward providing adequate notice as to the obligations and responsibilities involved with using the server and networking environments. If an investigator suspects a user during a forensic case, then the investigation against that user will clearly show that the individual's actions were intentional in nature. Warnings must be present at all of the access points in an organization if the organization wishes to prosecute an unauthorized user.

A warning banner should inform an authentic user when monitoring is being used to identify or watch an intruder (for example, if a hacker is downloading a user's file, keystroke monitoring will intercept both the hacker's download command and the authorized user's file).

A warning banner should also indicate when system administrators are monitoring authentic users during regular system maintenance.

The following are examples of common phrases on warning banners:

- "Access to this system and network is restricted."
- "Use of this system and network is for official business only."
- "Systems and networks are subject to monitoring at any time by the owner."
- "Using this system implies consent to monitoring by the owner."
- "Unauthorized or illegal users of this system or network will be subject to discipline or prosecution."

Collecting the Evidence

An investigator must seek permission to conduct a search at the site of a crime from the judiciary branch of that particular location. The investigator should look for evidence at the crime scene that may pertain to the case. A computer can be an excellent source of information that can be beneficial to the law enforcement agents involved in solving the case. Sometimes, computers and their related components can determine the chain of events leading up to a crime and can provide the evidence required for a conviction.

Obtaining a Search Warrant

An investigator can execute his or her investigation once the investigation plan has been developed. The investigator needs to first obtain a search warrant from a court. A *search warrant* is a written order issued by a judge that directs a law enforcement officer to search for a particular piece of evidence at a particular location. Successful computer search warrants should include the particular object the investigator wants to seize and the search strategy used in the investigation. These steps help the examiner focus and execute the search in the best way. Figure 3-2 shows an example of a search warrant.

Search Warrant Purview

Depending upon the circumstances of a case, a warrant can be issued for:

- An entire company
- A floor of a company building
- A room in a company building
- A device
- A car
- A house
- Any other company property

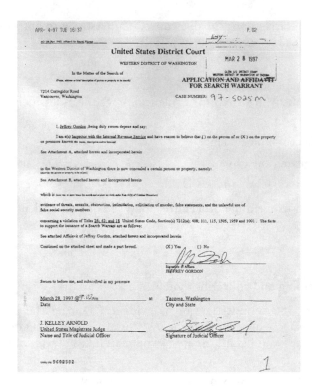 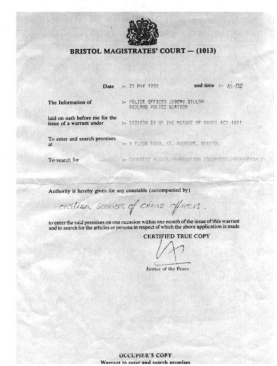

Figure 3-2 This is an example of a search warrant that has been obtained as part of an investigation.

The proposed warrant is basically a one-page form, along with attachments incorporated by reference, indicating the place to be searched and the persons or things to be seized. If the probable cause of search and the descriptions of the place to be searched and things to be seized are adequately established in the court, then the judge will sign the warrant. Under the federal rules of criminal procedure, execution of the warrant should take place within 10 days of the signing of the warrant.

Preparing for Searches

Prior to a judge issuing a search and seizure warrant for all or part of a target computer, an investigator needs to determine the computer's significance in the offense.

The role of a computer in an offense could be that it is:

1. *A tool of the offense*: For example, a counterfeiter might use his scanner and printer to scan and print currency. In this context, the computer is actively involved in performing illicit activity.

2. *A repository of the offense*: For example, an identity thief might stealthily store credit card details of customers.

   In certain situations, the computer is used as both a tool and a repository. For example, hackers can use a computer both to attack a system and to store stolen files.

Warrants should be issued with consideration to the role of the computer in the crime.

Searches Without a Warrant

In certain situations, searches performed without a warrant may be allowed. These special situations are identified below:

- "When destruction of evidence is imminent, a warrantless seizure of that evidence is justified if there is probable cause to believe that the item seized constitutes evidence of criminal activity." *United States v. David*, 756 F. Supp. 1385, 1392 (D. Nev. 1991)

- "Agents may search a place or object without a warrant or probable cause, if a person with authority has consented."*Schneckloth v. Bustamonte*, 412 U.S. 218, 219 (1973)

Performing a Preliminary Assessment

An investigator should perform a preliminary assessment to search for evidence. After the assessment is over, the investigator needs to perform the following steps:

1. Take a snapshot of the crime scene before collecting the evidence.
2. Collect and seize the equipment used in committing the crime.
3. Document the items collected, such as floppy disks, CDs, and DVDs.

After performing these steps, the investigator can document the procedures followed during evidence gathering and then begin the actual investigation.

Examining and Collecting Evidence

The following steps should be followed when examining and collecting evidence:

1. *Find the evidence*: The most important part of any investigation is evidence. During the gathering process, the investigator should look for the place where the evidence is stored. The investigator needs to prepare a checklist to cross-check the findings and list all the items that can be used for committing a crime.
2. *Discover the relevant data*: It should be clear to the investigator which data should be taken. It is a waste of time to gather unnecessary data. It is inadvisable to seize an entire system if it can be avoided. The investigator must first identify the relevant data and then gather it; otherwise, over-collection can result.
3. *Prepare an order of volatility*: Some evidence is volatile, which means it does not last long. Such evidence is called volatile evidence, as it needs a consistent power supply for storage or it contains information that is constantly changing.

   While gathering the evidence, the investigator should prepare an order of volatility to ensure that all relevant data are collected. The order should be from the most volatile to the least. The order of volatility functions as a guide that can help the investigator gather the evidence in the best order.

   Order of volatility can be:
   - Registers and cache
   - Routing tables
   - ARP cache
   - Process table
   - Kernel statistics and modules

Acquiring the Subject Evidence

An investigator needs to take several steps when acquiring evidence that he or she has identified as relevant to the case. According to the National Institute of Justice (2004), these steps are:

- Investigate the makeup of any storage device to ensure that all space is accounted for, including host-protected data areas (for example, ensuring that non-host-specific data such as the partition table matches the physical makeup of the drive).
- Capture the electronic serial number of the drive and other user-accessible, host-specific data.
- Obtain the evidence using the appropriate tools, including:
  - Stand-alone duplication software
  - Forensic analysis software suites
  - Dedicated hardware devices
- Using sector-by-sector comparison, correlate the values in the evidence and the backup.

Methods of Collecting Evidence

Evidence is collected from a live computer by searching the following:

- *Process register*: It includes services like calibration inspection and testing, construction management, hardware, and software.
- *Virtual and physical memory*: These provide a complete address space for every process and protect each process from other processes.
- *Network state*: It shows the state of the network and includes the IP address and URL.
- *Running processes*: These are all the processes currently running on the computer.
- *Disks, tapes, and CD-ROMs*: These are the physical media used for data storage.
- *Paper printouts*: These show data that have been printed out from a live computer.

The following are the volatile sources and commands used to capture the evidence on live computers:

- *ps or the /proc file system*: Used to run the processes
- *netstat*: Displays active TCP connections, Ethernet statistics, and the IP routing table
- *arp (ARP cache)*: Displays the mappings between different layers of the network architecture
- *lsof (list of open files)*: Shows all the files that are currently open
- */dev/mem and /dev/kmem*: Examines each and every patch in the computer

The following are the computer forensic tools used for data collection:

- Guidance Software's EnCase (*www.guidancesoftware.com*); EnCase is a forensic data and analysis program for various operating systems that is used to perform computer-related investigation. Using EnCase, an investigator can quickly find files that have been misplaced or deleted. It also allows an investigator to understand and define the information present in a system.
- AccessData's Forensic Toolkit (*www.accessdata.com*); AccessData's Forensic Toolkit, referred to by forensic analysts simply as FTK, contains the full suite of password recovery tools, drive and media wipers, a registry viewer, and other useful products. The password recovery tools also unlock locked files. Experts have found that people often use repeated passwords, which helps hackers gain access to systems. This software also enables access to password management, which manages and analyzes multiple files. Forensic Toolkit also enables the recovery of multilingual passwords, thus enabling the investigator to bypass security against the unauthorized access of these files.

Securing the Computer Evidence

The first step an investigator must take after identifying a security incident and collecting the evidence is to secure the evidence to prevent tampering. Securing the evidence involves retrieving all the information held on a computer so that it can be used in the investigation. The term *computer* here includes *all* computer media (for example, floppy disks, tapes, CD-ROMs, DVDs, and removable hard drives).

By securing the evidence, the investigator ensures that it is not altered during the examination process. Securing the evidence should be in accordance with best practices. **Best practices** are an empirically proven set of methods for performing a task in the best and most efficient way. If security is breached, the evidence might lose its credibility.

Taking the Necessary Steps

Because digital evidence can be easily tampered with, altered, or destroyed, an investigator needs to ensure that the evidence is preserved and secured well. Failure to do so may result in the evidence being inadmissible when submitted to a court of law.

An investigator needs to take the following steps to secure the digital evidence while collecting it at the crime scene:

- Follow departmental guidelines when possible; otherwise, use *A Guide for First Responders*.
- Document and verify the hardware configuration of the system to be examined.

- Disassemble the computer to be examined.
- Identify and document the internal storage devices.

Preventing Evidence Tampering

It is essential for the investigator to ensure that the least amount of tampering is done to the evidence, because tampering can alter the evidence. To do so, the investigator must prevent anyone from tampering with the evidence, either remotely or at the suspect system.

1. *Gather the evidence*: Gather the evidence using appropriate and industry-accepted techniques and procedures.

2. *Prepare the chain of custody*: The investigator must document the gathering process. The document should include time stamps, digital signatures, and signed statements. An investigator must never turn on or operate the subject computer during an investigation. If the subject computer has to be on, the investigator should unplug the system and make sure it is not connected to the network environment.

Processing Location Assessment

The investigator who is examining the evidence needs to decide the best place to examine the evidence after accessing it. An environment such as a dedicated forensic work area or laboratory is recommended. It is also recommended to control the environment in case the examination is conducted onsite.

Assessment considerations might include the following:

- The time required to recover the evidence when onsite
- Logistic and workforce concerns related to long-term deployment
- Business impact of a time-consuming search
- The suitability of equipment, resources, media, training, and experience for an onsite examination

Chain-of-Evidence Form

The chain-of-evidence form documents what has and has not been done with both the original evidence and any forensic copies of the evidence. Figure 3-3 shows a typical chain-of-evidence form.

The information contained in such a form, including some not shown in the example, is explained below:

- *Case number*: The number of the case being investigated. Each case has a different case number, and this number is assigned by the organization to which an investigator belongs.
- *Investigating organization*: The name of the organization investigating the case.
- *Investigator for the case*: The name of the investigator who is dealing with the case. It may happen that a certain case requires more than one investigator; in such cases, this field contains the name of the lead investigator.
- *Nature of the case*: A short description of the case. If an employee violates the company policy, then the nature of the case is "Employee Policy Violation Case."
- *Description of the evidence*: Contains information about the type of evidence collected.
- *Evidence recovered by*: The name of the investigator who recovered the evidence. This is the building block for chain of custody. **Chain of custody** is a method of documenting the history and possession of a sample from the time of its collection to its final disposition. It is the responsibility of the person who recovers the evidence to ensure that nothing damages the evidence and no one tampers with it. The investigator is responsible for the transportation, security, and preservation of evidence.
- *Date and time*: The date and time when the evidence was taken into custody.
- *Location from which the evidence was recovered*: The location where the evidence was discovered. In the case of multiple pieces of evidence, a new form is created for each different location.
- *Evidence processed by item number*: When the evidence is processed and analyzed by an investigator, the name of the person who handled and processed it on a particular date and time is written here.

Date	Type of Incident	Case#
Consent Required Y/N	Signature of Consenting Person	Tag#
Model#	Manufacturer#	Serial#
Description of Form		
Person Receiving Evidence	Signature	

Chain of Custody			
From	Date	Reason	To
Location			Location
From	Date	Reason	To
Location			Location
From	Date	Reason	To
Location			Location
From	Date	Reason	To
Location			Location
From	Date	Reason	To
Location			Location
Final Disposition of Evidence	Date		

Figure 3-3 This is a chain-of-evidence form, which documents all that has been done to a particular piece of evidence.

- *Evidence placed in the locker*: Contains information about which secure evidence container is being used to store the evidence and when the evidence was placed in it.
- *Item/evidence processed by/Disposition of evidence/Date/Time*: Contains information regarding the investigator name, specific item number of evidence, and description about what was performed when an investigator obtains the evidence for processing and analysis.
- *Page number*: Contains the page number of the form. The page number is specified in the format "Page *x* of *y*."
- *Name of vendor*: The name of the manufacturer of the evidence. For example, if the evidence is a floppy disk, its manufacturer could be Imation or IBM.
- *Model or serial number*: The model number or serial number of the computer component. Most computer components have model numbers rather than serial numbers. Single pieces of computer equipment can have different model numbers, and as technology is upgraded, new features are added to existing equipment.

Examining the Digital Evidence

The investigator should perform the examination process on a bit-stream copy rather than on the original computer. While writing up documentation, the investigator must use an accurate system date and time. Inaccurate time and date information can change the whole case and can also contribute to losing the case because of inaccurate information.

Understanding Bit-Stream Copies

An important factor in evidence retrieval is how exact a copy of evidence is, because the more exact the copy, the better the chances are of retrieving the evidence from the disk. To meet this need, bit-stream copy comes into play.

Creating a bit-stream image transfers each bit of data from the original disk to the same spot on the image disk

Original disk   Image disk   Target disk

Transfer of data from original to bit-stream image to target

Figure 3-4   This shows what a bit-stream copy is and how one is made.

A *bit-stream copy* is a bit-by-bit copy of the original storage medium (Figure 3-4). That's why it is different from a simple backup copy of a disk. A bit-stream copy is an exact duplicate of the original disk, while a backup copy is nothing but a compressed file stored in a folder. Bit-streaming can create an exact image of a disk, as it is copied bit-by-bit.

Creating a Bit-Stream Copy

A bit-stream image is a file that contains a duplicate copy of all the data on a disk or disk partition. To create a bit-stream image of an evidence disk, an investigator should copy the bit-stream image to a target work disk, which is identical in all aspects to the evidence disk. Before copying the disk, the investigator must ensure that the disk used for copying is similar (in other words, the manufacturer and model of the target disk must be the same as the manufacturer and model of the original evidence disk). Although some software tools that create bit-stream images can accommodate a target disk of a different size, it is better to have the same size disks.

The computer is used only when the bit-stream copies of the disk drives and floppy disks are made.

Imaging

The investigator should analyze the duplicate copy of any evidence so that the original evidence will not be altered, because the first rule of forensic science is to preserve the original evidence. Once the investigator has made a copy of the original data, the copy should be used for further processing. The original should not be touched.

To create a forensic copy of a floppy disk, which is an exact duplicate of the original disk, the investigator should make a bit-stream data copy employing an MS-DOS command or specialized tool, such as the Digital Intelligence Image utility. Before creating the copy, the investigator should retrieve the floppy disk from the secure evidence container and provide the appropriate information on the evidence form.

The forensic copy can be created using various techniques, such as:

- Using MS-DOS to create a bit-stream copy of a floppy disk
- Using Image to acquire a bit-stream copy of a floppy disk
- Using Image to make a bit-stream copy of the evidence

Making a Bit-Stream Copy Using MS-DOS

1. First, write-protect the floppy by moving the write-protect tab to the open position.
2. Insert the evidence disk into the disk drive.
3. Type **diskcopy A: A: /V** at the MS-DOS prompt and press Enter. /V is a verification switch to verify that the data is copied correctly.
4. When the disk is copied, remove the evidence disk, insert the target disk, and proceed with the data copy following the on-screen instructions.
5. Type **N** for no if a message either to create another duplicate of the disk or to copy another disk appears.

6. Return the evidence disk to the secure container.

7. Put the label **Domain Name working copy#1** on the target disk.

Acquiring a Bit-Stream Copy of a Floppy Disk Using Image

1. Write-protect the floppy by moving the write-protect tab to the open position.

2. Insert the evidence disk into the disk drive.

3. At the command prompt, type **cd \work folder\Folder\Subfolder**, where **work folder** is the root directory and **Folder** is below the root. Press Enter.

4. To acquire data from the evidence disk, type **image a: c:\work folder\Folder\Subfolder\evidence.img** and press Enter.

5. Return the evidence disk to the secure container.

6. A bit-stream copy of the disk is stored in a file called **evidence.img** on the hard disk.

7. The next step is to transfer the image to a target disk to create a forensic copy.

Making a Bit-Stream Copy of Evidence Using Image

1. Navigate to **My Computer** to find the **evidence.img** file in the **Folder\Subfolder** data files.

2. Copy the **evidence.img** file from data files to the **Folder\Subfolder** on the hard disk.

3. At the command prompt, type **cd \work folder\Folder\Subfolder** and press Enter.

4. Insert the target disk in the disk drive.

5. Type **image evidence.img a:** and press Enter.

6. Put the label **Testing Copy** on the target disk.

   While transferring the data of the image file, Image decompresses the image file and creates an exact duplicate of the disk. It also includes slack space and free space on the disk. *Slack space* is the space that exists between the end of a file and the end of the last cluster used by that file (the end of the allotted space for a file), and free space is the space not reserved for saved files.

Write Protection

According to the National Institute of Justice (2004), write protection should be initiated, if available, to preserve and protect original evidence.

The examiner should consider creating a known value for the subject evidence prior to acquiring the evidence (for example, performing an independent cyclic redundancy check [CRC] or using MD5 hashing). Depending on the selected acquisition method, this process may have already been completed.

- If hardware write protection is used:
  - Install a write-protection device.
  - Boot the system with the examiner's controlled operating system.
- If software write protection is used:
  - Boot the system with the examiner's controlled operating system.
  - Activate write protection.

Retrieving Deleted Files

After committing a crime, a criminal usually tries to remove all traces of the crime, and while doing it, the criminal deletes the files he or she used. When an investigation starts, the purpose of analyzing digital evidence is to recover these files. When files are deleted, the space they occupied becomes free space. These files can be recovered if the free space is not overwritten with a new file. The forensic tool used to retrieve such files is the MS-DOS tool from Digital Intelligence called DriveSpy. This tool is a command-line tool.

What Is DriveSpy?

DriveSpy is a disk-forensic DOS tool designed to emulate and extend the capabilities of DOS to meet forensic needs. The tool is compact enough to fit on a floppy disk.

It creates direct disk-to-disk forensic duplicates and can copy a range of sectors within or between drives and process duplicate drives regardless of physical drive geometry or sector translation differences. DriveSpy uses familiar DOS commands (cd, dir, and others) to navigate the system under investigation and, if needed, extend the capabilities of the associated DOS commands or add new commands. It searches for, analyzes, and extracts data from floppy disks or hard disks. It is capable of reading disk drives greater than 8.4 GB in size and disk partitions greater than 2 GB in size in systems running MS-DOS version 6.22.

DriveSpy operates in one of the following modes:

- *System mode*: Operates at the BIOS level and permits the navigation and viewing of all disk drives connected to the computer

- *Drive mode*: Used while examining an unformatted disk; accesses the physical level, which allows viewing the raw data on a disk

- *Part mode*: Also known as partition mode; refers to the logical structure of the disk and can show the directory and files for the file allocation table (FAT)

How to Use Digital Intelligence DriveSpy DriveSpy records all activities to a log file. It recovers and analyzes data on FAT12, FAT16, FAT16x, and FAT32 partitions. DriveSpy identifies hard disks by number, with the first drive being DOS, but it does not number the floppy disk and CD-ROM drives. To launch DriveSpy, DriveSpy.exe must be in the same folder as the DriveSpy.ini and DriveSpy.hlp files.

Preparing to Analyze a Bit-Stream Copy of an Evidence Disk Using DriveSpy

1. Write-protect the floppy disk by moving the notch to the open position.
2. Boot the workstation to MS-DOS.
3. Run the Toolpath.bat command.
4. Insert the Testing Copy into the disk drive.

   The system is now ready to start DriveSpy.

Analyzing a Bit-Stream Copy of an Evidence Disk Using DriveSpy

1. Type **DriveSpy** at the **MS-DOS** prompt and press Enter.
2. At the **SYS>** prompt, run the following command: **output workfolder\Folder\Subfolder\evidence.log**
3. To access the evidence disk, type **Drive A** and press Enter.
4. DriveSpy opens in disk mode.
5. Run command **Part 1** at the **DA** prompt to access partition mode.
6. Type **Q** to exit.

Extracting the Data

1. Restart DriveSpy.
2. Run the following command at the **SYS>** prompt: **output workfolder\Folder\Subfolder\Evidence.log**
3. To access drive mode, type **Drive A** and press Enter.
4. To switch to partition mode, run **Part 1** at the **DA** prompt.
5. At the **DAP1** prompt, run the following command: **dbexport workfolder\Folder\Subfolder\Evidence.txt**
6. Run the following command to copy all the allocated data: **copy *.* /S workfolder\Folder\Subfolder**
7. Press **Y** to view the results in page mode.
8. Type **unerase *.* /S workfolder\Folder\Subfolder** and press Enter.

DriveSpy searches the FAT for all deleted files having a lowercase sigma (σ) and copies the deleted data into the location called "Folder" in the work folder.

Analyzing the Data

1. Reboot the machine into Windows mode.
2. Navigate to **My Computer** to view the files on the floppy disk.
3. Right-click the first file, and click **Properties**.
4. Note the properties of each file, such as the creation, modification, and access dates and times in a separate document of Notepad.
5. Use **My Computer** to open **work folder\Folder\Subfolder** to examine the content of each file.
6. Open **Evidence.txt** in Notepad and examine the contents.
7. Examine the contents of all the deleted files.
8. Disconnect storage devices to avoid damage or alteration of data.

Evidence Assessment

The investigator must consider the following while assessing the evidence:

- Prioritizing the evidence:
  - Location of evidence at the crime scene
  - Stability of media to be examined
- Establishing how to document the evidence (for example, photographs, sketches, or notes)
- Evaluating storage locations for electromagnetic interference
- Determining the state of the evidence after packaging, transport, or storage
- Evaluating the necessity to provide a continuous power supply to battery-operated devices

Evidence Examination

For digital evidence, forensic principles are generally enforced. The National Institute of Justice (2004) describes these principles. Depending on the type of case and media, the corresponding examination methodologies are used. Proper training must be given to those who conduct examinations.

For conducting examinations, examiners must:

- Use accepted forensic procedures.
- Avoid using the original evidence.

Analysis of recovered data involves interpreting the data and putting it into a logical and useful format (for example, determining how the evidence got there, what it means, and where it came from). Analysis is the phase in which acquired data turns to evidence. When conducting the evidence examination, the following steps should be taken into consideration:

- *Preparation*: This allows the investigator to prepare the working directory or directories on separate media so that evidentiary files and data can be recovered or extracted.
- *Extraction*: There are two different types of extraction, physical and logical. The physical extraction phase identifies and recovers the data across the entire physical drive without regard to the file system. The logical extraction phase identifies and recovers files and data based on installed operating system(s), file system(s), and/or application(s).

Physical Extraction

During this stage, extraction of data from the drive occurs at the physical level, regardless of the file systems present on the drive. This may include the following methods:

- Keyword searching, file carving, and extraction of the partition table and unused space on the physical drive.

- Performing a keyword search across the physical drive; this may be useful, as it allows the examiner to extract data that may not be accounted for by the operating system and file system.

- File-carving utilities processed across the physical drive; this may assist in recovering and extracting usable files and data that may not be accounted for by the operating system and file system.

- Examining the partition structure; this may identify the file systems present and determine if the entire physical size of the hard drive is accounted for.

Logical Extraction

During this stage, the extraction of the data from the drive is based on the file system(s) present on the drive and may include data from such areas as active files, deleted files, file slack, and unallocated file space. *File slack* is the space that exists between the end of the file and the end of the last cluster used by that file.

Steps may include:

- Extraction of the file system information to reveal characteristics such as directory structure, file attributes, file names, date and time stamps, file size, and file location

- Data reduction to identify and eliminate known files through the comparison of calculated hash values to authenticated hash values

- Extraction of files pertinent to the examination; methods to accomplish this may be based on file name and extension, file header, file content, and location on the drive

- Recovery of deleted files

- Extraction of password-protected, encrypted, and compressed data

- Extraction of file slack

- Extraction of unallocated space

Analysis of Extracted Data

Depending on the file system on the drives, data is extracted from:

- Active files
- Deleted files
- File slack
- Unallocated file space

The data extracted above is used to find the following information:

- Directory structure
- File attributes
- File names
- Date and time stamps
- File size
- File location

Thus, analysis involves examining the extracted data to resolve the critical consequences of the case, if any. A few characteristics of the data that can be analyzed are:

- Time frame
- Data hiding
- Application and file
- Ownership and possession

Analysis may require the following:

- A review of the request for service
- Legal authority for a search of the digital evidence

- Investigative leads
- Analytical leads

Time-Frame Analysis

In situations where an individual is suspected of using a certain computer, time-frame analysis can contribute to associating the events that occurred on the computer with that individual.

Time-frame analysis can be performed using two methods:

1. The first involves reviewing the time stamps and date stamps that are found in the file system metadata (for example, when the files were last modified, last accessed, created, or changed status). These clues might provide useful details to further the investigation. An example of this analysis would be using the last modified date and time to establish when the contents of a file were last changed.

2. The second method involves reviewing the application logs that are found (the logs may include the error logs, installation logs, connection logs, and security logs). For example, examination of a security log may indicate when a user name/password combination was used to log in to a system.

 Take into consideration any differences in the individual's computer date and time as reported in the BIOS.

Data-Hiding Analysis

Data can be hidden on the storage devices of the computer. To detect and recover such information that is hidden, data-hiding analysis contributes to revealing the knowledge, ownership, or intent contained therein.

Data-hiding analysis is performed in the following ways:

1. Identifying mismatches between the file headers and the file extensions; the presence of a mismatch indicates a malicious intent to conceal data.

2. Attempting to access all password-protected, encrypted, and compressed files, indicating that an illegitimate user has or has tried to conceal the data from unauthorized users; a password itself may be as relevant as the contents of the file.

3. Using steganography; *steganography* is the art and process of hiding information by embedding messages in other, seemingly harmless messages.

Any attempt to hide data can be revealed through the discovery of user-created data in a host-protected area. A *host-protected area (HPA)* is an area of the drive where a certain portion of the drive's contents is hidden from the operating system and file system.

Application and File Analysis

The results of application and file analysis may provide important details, such as the proficiency of the user and the system's capabilities. These results may show that additional steps need to be taken, such as:

- Reviewing file names for relevance and patterns
- Examining file content
- Identifying the number and types of operating systems
- Correlating the files to the applications installed on the target computer
- Looking for similarities between files
- Correlating Internet history to cache files, and e-mail files to e-mail attachments
- Identifying unknown file types to determine their value to the investigation
- Identifying the presence of files in storage locations other than the locations where the files are usually stored for a particular application
- Examining user-configuration settings
- Analyzing file metadata, which is additional data that is attached to a user-created file and containing information that is not usually presented to the user but that can typically be viewed through the application used to create it

Ownership and Possession

In certain cases, the examiner may need to identify the user(s) who created, modified, or accessed a file. The ownership details of the data being sought might be critical in the analyses described above. Certain factors, such as the ones mentioned below, determine the knowledgeable possession of data:

- Placing the subject at the computer on a particular date and at a specific time can help identify the ownership and possession of the concealed or modified data.

- The presence of files at locations other than the default indicates that they might be of investigative value. Using application and file analysis can identify this.

- At times, the file itself may contain ownership details that might be of evidentiary value. Using application and file analysis can identify this.

- The presence of concealed data indicates an intentional attempt to mislead an investigator by avoiding detection. Using hidden data analysis can identify this.

- Recovering the password-protected or encrypted files might reveal the possession of the files. Using hidden data analysis can identify this.

- Ownership details of the file may at times be contained within the file itself. Using application and file analysis can identify this.

Documenting and Reporting

Reporting the results of analysis and the steps taken during analysis of the digital evidence is a major responsibility of the investigator. Every step of the investigation must be documented to retain the flow of the investigative steps, digital evidence collection, and examination.

An investigator must document everything. Documentation should be a continuous process that records the entire process of examination completely and accurately. It should be readable, and the report should appropriately address the intended audience. The investigator should take the following steps during the documentation process:

- Take notes when consulting with the case investigator and/or prosecutor.

- Maintain a copy of the search authority with the case notes.

- Maintain the initial request for assistance with the case file.

- Maintain a copy of chain-of-custody documentation.

- Take notes detailed enough to allow complete duplication of actions.

- Include in the notes the dates, times, and descriptions and results of actions taken.

- Document irregularities encountered and any actions taken regarding irregularities during the examination.

- Include additional information, such as network topology, a list of authorized users, user agreements, and passwords.

- Document changes made to the system or network by or at the direction of law enforcement or the examiner.

- Document the operating system, relevant software versions, and current installed patches.

- Document information obtained at the scene regarding remote storage, remote user access, and offsite backups.

Certain information that may help in furthering the investigation might be identified during the process of examination. This might be beyond the scope of the current legal authority. The investigator should document this so that an additional search warrant can be obtained.

The Final Report

The final report should consist of the findings of the investigation in detail. The report should include:

- Specific files related to the request

- Other files, including hidden and deleted files that support the findings

Maintaining Professional Conduct

An investigator should follow these rules in order to maintain professional conduct while investigating a case:

- Contribute to society and behave well.
- Avoid harming others.
- Be honest and trustworthy.
- Be fair and do not discriminate.
- Honor property rights, copyrights, and patent rights.
- Give appropriate credit for intellectual property.
- Respect the privacy of others.
- Honor confidentiality.
- Maintain effectiveness and dignity at all times during an investigation.
- Acquire and maintain professional competence.
- Respect the existing laws pertaining to professional work.
- Accept and provide appropriate professional review.
- Consider all the available facts that relate to the crime scene.
- Avoid external biases to maintain the integrity of the fact finding in all investigations.
- Keep the case confidential.
- Update the computer hardware and software, networking, and forensic tools with the latest technology.
- Maintain the chain of custody.
- Give inclusive and thorough evaluations of computer systems and their impacts, including analyses of possible risks.
- Honor contracts, agreements, and assigned responsibilities.
- Improve public understanding of computing and its consequences.
- Access computing and communication resources only when permission is granted.
- Supervise personnel and resources in order to design and build information systems that improve the quality of working life.
- Acknowledge and support proper and authorized users of an organization's computing and communication resources.
- Conduct sessions in the organization to know about the principles and limitations of computer systems.

- String searches, keyword searches, and text string searches
- Evidence found relating to the use or abuse of the Internet, such as Web site traffic analysis, chat logs, cache files, e-mail, newsgroup activity, and Internet history
- Graphic image analysis
- Indicators of ownership, which could include program registration data

- Data analysis
- Descriptions of relevant applications on the examined items
- Techniques used to hide or mask data, such as encryption, steganography, hidden attributes, hidden partitions, and file name anomalies
- Supporting materials, such as the chain-of-custody documentation, digital copies of evidence, and print-outs of specific evidence

Closing the Case

Once the evidence has been analyzed and retrieved, the investigator needs to prepare a final report. This report should include everything the investigator did during the course of the investigation and what he or she found. Basic reports should include who, what, when, where, and how. In a good computing investigation, the steps are repeatable and always produce the same results. The report should explain the computer and network processes and should include the log files generated by the forensic tools to keep track of all the steps taken.

The investigator should document all of the proceedings related to the investigation so that the documentation can be used as proof of findings in a court of law. Since the reader can be a senior personnel manager, a lawyer, or a judge, the investigator needs to provide a complete explanation of the various processes and the inner workings of the system and its various interrelated components.

Each organization has its own predefined template for report writing. The investigator should follow the template and understand the organization's needs and requirements when describing the findings. Log files generated by the forensic tools should be attached to the formal report, as they can be used in court to support the findings of the evidence.

Chapter Summary

- Securing computer evidence is the process by which all information held on a computer is retrieved to aid an investigation.
- An organization's banner should give clear and unequivocal notice to intruders that by signing on to the system, they are expressly consenting to monitoring.
- A bit-stream copy is a bit-by-bit copy of the original storage medium and an *exact* copy of the original disk.
- Examining the evidence depends on the type of case and the digital media available at the crime scene.
- Digital evidence should be thoroughly assessed with respect to the scope of the case to determine the course of action.
- Analysis is the process of interpreting the extracted data to determine their significance to the case.

Review Questions

1. Explain the basic steps in computer investigation.

_____

_____

2. Discuss the policy and procedure development stage of computer investigation.

_____

_____

3. Describe the various computer investigation methodologies.

_____

_____

4. Does an investigator need a search warrant to carry out an investigation?

_____

_____

5. What do warning banners help a user understand?

_____

_____

6. How do you collect evidence?

_____

_____

7. Explain the various methods of examining digital evidence.

_____

_____

8. How do you evaluate a case on the basis of evidence?

_____

_____

9. Write in detail about evidence assessment.

_____

_____

10. Write in detail about what is involved in a company policy violation.

_____

_____

11. How do you obtain a search warrant?

_____

_____

Hands-On Projects

1. Design a warning banner for a fictional organization. The banner should alert legitimate users that they can be monitored at any time. Compare and contrast this banner to the description of warning banners in this chapter.

2. Design a chain-of-evidence form that contains all the information necessary for keeping track of evidence during an investigation. Compare and contrast your chain-of-evidence form with the one in this chapter.

3. Follow these steps:

   ■ Navigate to Chapter 3 of the Student Resource Center.

   ■ Extract Decode.zip.

   ■ Open a command shell. Figure 3-5 shows this command shell.

   ■ Type dcode.exe to launch the application. Figure 3-6 shows what the application looks like.

   ■ Type 40B3B13FED2AC001 as the value to decode (this is a random sample value). Figure 3-7 shows the result of the decoding.

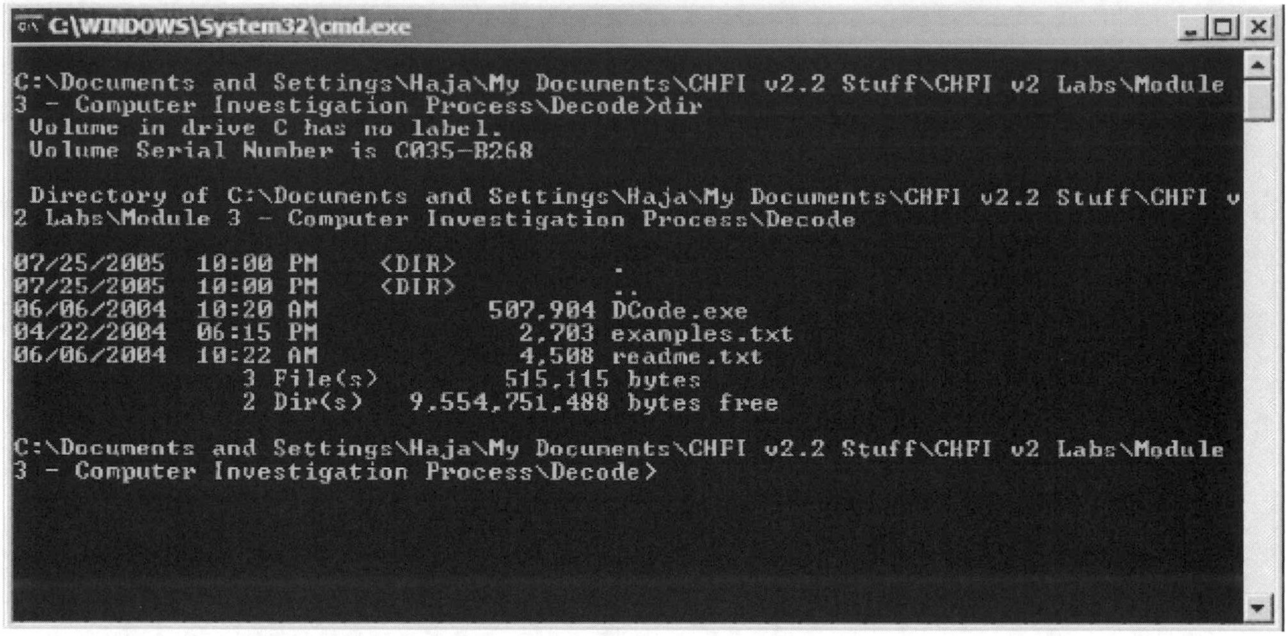

Figure 3-5   This is a command shell listing the contents of Decode.zip.

Figure 3-6   This is a screenshot of the DCode Date program.

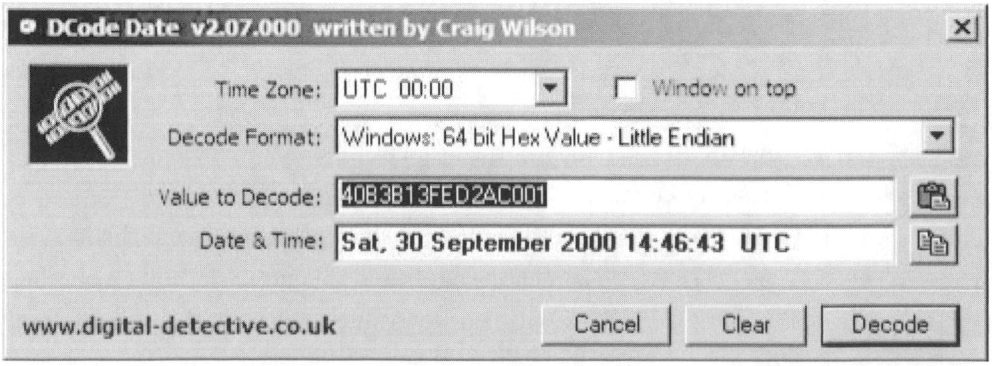

Figure 3-7   This screenshot shows the result of decoding the hex value you entered.

4. Follow these steps:

   ■ Navigate to Chapter 3 of the Student Resource Center.

   ■ Read the document titled "How to develop an effective response to subpoenas and search.pdf."

   ■ Read the document titled "challenge-of-the-forensic-investigation-of-computer-crime.pdf."

   ■ Read the document titled "Search Warrant upon Oral Testimony.pdf."

References

National Institute of Justice. (2004). Forensic examination of digital evidence: A guide for law enforcement. Retrieved from http://www.ncjrs.gov/pdffiles1/nij/199408.pdf

Chapter 4

First Responder Procedures

Objectives

After completing this chapter, you should be able to:

- Understand electronic evidence
- Understand the role of the first responder
- Recognize types of electronic devices and collect them as potential evidence
- Build a first responder toolkit
- Understand evidence-collecting tools and equipment
- Follow first responder procedures
- Secure and evaluate electronic crime scenes
- Conduct preliminary interviews
- Document electronic crime scenes
- Collect and preserve electronic evidence
- Package electronic evidence
- Transport electronic evidence
- Create reports about crime scenes
- Avoid some common mistakes of first responders

Key Terms

360-degree photographs   overlapping photographs showing the entire crime scene

Volatility   the measure of how perishable electronically stored data are

Case Example

Sam, a system administrator, is surprised to see critical files missing from his office server. He suspects that the server is compromised so he reports the incident to Bob, an information security officer employed with the same firm. As a certified forensic investigator, Bob knows exactly how to properly seize Sam's system and follow the basic procedures for investigating the case.

Bob investigates an imaged file of the server's hard disk. His investigation reveals the presence of a rootkit placed in one of the directories on the server. During the investigation process, Sam told Bob that he recalled downloading a patch management tool from a third-party source on the Internet. The rootkit could have been bundled with this tool.

Introduction to First Responder Procedures

The term *first responder* refers to a person who first arrives at a crime scene and accesses the victim's computer system once the incident has been reported. The first responder may be a network administrator, law enforcement officer, or investigating officer. Generally, the first responder is a person who comes from the forensic laboratory or from a particular agency for initial investigation.

If a crime occurs that affects a company's servers or individual workstations, the company first contacts the forensic laboratory or agency for crime investigation. The laboratory or agency then sends the first responder to the crime scene for initial investigation. The first responder is responsible for protecting, integrating, and preserving the evidence obtained from the crime scene.

The first responder needs to have complete knowledge of computer forensic investigation procedures. He or she preserves all evidence in a simple, protected, and forensically sound manner. The first responder must investigate the crime scene in a lawful manner so that any obtained evidence will be acceptable in a court of law.

Electronic Evidence

Electronic evidence is data relevant to an investigation that is transferred by or stored on an electronic device. This type of evidence is found when data on any physical device is collected for examination. Electronic evidence has the following properties:

- It may be hidden, similar to fingerprint evidence or DNA evidence.
- It can be broken, changed, damaged, or cracked by improper handling; therefore, particular precautions must be taken to document, gather, safeguard, and examine these types of evidences.
- It can expire after a period of time.

Sources of Electronic Evidence

Electronic information is usually stored on magnetic or optical storage devices, such as floppy disks, flash drives, memory cards, backup tapes, CD-ROMs, and DVD-ROMs. Hard drives, including removable drives and laptop drives, often contain significant information in hidden files.

Computer systems—in particular PCs and network servers in which electronic data are organized, stored, deleted, and accessed—should not be ignored. All e-mail servers and their backup schedules are also critical, and any Internet-related files should be obtained from Internet service providers or specific network servers.

Role of the First Responder

As the first person to arrive at the crime scene, the first responder plays an important role in computer forensic investigation. After all the evidence is collected from the crime scene, the investigation process starts. If the evidence collected by the first responder is forensically sound, it is significantly easier for the investigation team to find the actual cause of the crime.

The following are the main responsibilities of the first responder:

- *Identifying the crime scene*: After arriving at the crime scene, the first responder identifies the scope of the crime scene and establishes a perimeter. The perimeter will include a particular area, room, several rooms, or even an entire building, depending on whether the computers are networked. The first responder should list the computer systems involved in the incident.
- *Protecting the crime scene*: Like any other case, a search warrant is required for the search and seizure of digital and electronic evidence. Therefore, the first responder should protect all computers and electronic devices while waiting for the officer in charge.
- *Preserving temporary and fragile evidence*: In the case of temporary and fragile evidence that could change or disappear, such as screen information and running programs, the first responder does not wait for the officer in charge. Rather, he or she takes immediate photographs of this evidence.

- *Collecting all information about the incident*: The first responder conducts preliminary interviews of all persons present at the crime scene and asks questions about the incident.

- *Documenting all findings*: The first responder starts documenting all information about the collected evidence in the chain of custody document. The chain of custody document contains information such as case number, name and title of the individual from whom the report is received, address and telephone number, location where the evidence is obtained, date and time when the evidence is obtained, and a complete description of each item.

- *Packaging and transporting the electronic evidence*: After collecting the evidence, the first responder labels all the evidence and places it in evidence storage bags, which protect it from sunlight and extreme temperatures. These bags also block wireless signals so that wireless devices cannot acquire data from the evidence. The storage bags are then transported to the forensic laboratory.

Electronic Devices: Types and Collecting Potential Evidence

The following are some of the types of electronic devices relevant to a crime scene:

- *Computer systems*: A computer system generally consists of the central processing unit (CPU), motherboard, memory, case, data storage devices, monitor, keyboard, and mouse. Digital evidence is found in files that are stored on memory cards, hard drives, USB drives, other removable storage devices, and media such as floppy disks, CDs, DVDs, cartridges, and tapes.

- *Hard drives*: A hard drive is an electronic storage device that stores data magnetically.

- *Thumb drives*: A thumb drive is a removable data storage device with a USB connection.

- *Memory cards*: A memory card is a removable electronic storage device that is used in many devices such as digital cameras, computers, and PDAs.

- *Smart cards, dongles, and biometric scanners*: Evidence is found in the data on the card or inside the devices themselves.

- *Answering machines*: These store voice messages, time and date information, and when messages were left. To find the evidence, an investigator should check the voice recordings for deleted messages, most recent numbers called, messages, recorded phone numbers, and tapes or digital recording data.

- *Digital cameras*: To find the evidence, an investigator should check the stored images, removable media, and time and date stamps of the images.

- *MP3 players*: To find the evidence, an investigator should check the information stored on the device.

- *Pagers*: To find the evidence, an investigator should check the stored addresses, text messages, e-mails, voice messages, and phone numbers.

- *Personal digital assistants*: PDAs are handheld devices that have computing, telephone or fax, paging, and networking features. To find the evidence, an investigator should check the address book, meeting calendar, documents, and e-mails.

- *Printers*: To find the evidence, an investigator should check the usage logs, time and date information, and network identity information.

- *Removable storage devices (tapes, CDs, DVDs, and floppies)*: Evidence is found on the devices themselves.

- *Telephones*: To find the evidence, an investigator should check stored names, stored phone numbers, and caller identification information.

- *Modems*: Evidence is found on the devices themselves.

- *Scanners*: Evidence is found in user usage logs and time and date stamps.

- *Copiers*: Evidence is found in user texts, user usage logs, and time and date stamps.

- *Credit card skimmers*: To find the evidence, an investigator should check the card expiration date, user's address, card numbers, and user's name.

- *Fax machines*: To find the evidence, an investigator should check the documents, phone numbers, film cartridges, and sent and received logs.

First Responder Toolkit

The first responder has to create a toolkit before a cybercrime event happens and prior to any potential evidence collection. Once a crime is reported, someone should immediately report to the site and should not have to waste any time gathering materials.

The first responder toolkit is a set of tested tools designed to help in collecting genuine presentable evidence. It helps the first responder understand the limitations and capabilities of electronic evidence at the time of collection. The act of creating a toolkit makes the first responder familiar with computer forensic tools and their functionalities.

The first responder has to select trusted computer forensic tools that provide output-specific information and determine system dependencies. For example, any program running on the victim's computer generally uses common libraries for routine system commands. If the first responder starts collecting evidence with the trusted tools, it will be easy to determine the system dependencies.

Creating a First Responder Toolkit

Creating a first responder toolkit includes the following procedures:

1. *Create a trusted forensic computer or test bed*: This trusted forensic computer or test bed will be used to test the functionality of the collected tools. Prior to testing any tool, the investigator should make sure that this is a trusted resource.

    To create a trusted forensic computer, follow these steps:

    -   Choose the operating system type. Create two different test bed machines: one for Windows and one for Linux.

    -   Completely sanitize the forensic computer. This includes formatting the hard disk completely to remove any data, using software such as BCWipe for Windows or Wipe for Linux.

    -   Install the operating system and required software from trusted resources. If the operating system is downloaded, verify the hashes prior to installation.

    -   Update and patch the forensic computer.

    -   Install a file integrity monitor to test the integrity of the file system.

2. *Document the details of the forensic computer*: Documenting the forensic computer or test bed is the second step in creating a first responder toolkit. It helps the forensic expert easily understand the situation and the tools used, and will help to reproduce results if they come into question for any reason.

    The forensic computer or test bed documentation should include the following:

    -   Version name and type of the operating system

    -   Names and types of the different software

    -   Names and types of the installed hardware

3. *Document the summary of collected tools*: The third step in creating a first responder toolkit is to document the summary of the collected tools. This allows the first responder to become more familiar with and understand the working of each tool.

    Information about the following should be included while documenting the summary of tools:

    -   Acquisition of the tool

    -   Detailed description of the tool

    -   Working of the tool

    -   Tool dependencies and system effects

4. *Test the tools*: After documenting the summary of the collected tools, the investigator should test them on the forensic computer or test bed to examine the performance and output. He or she should examine the effects of each tool on the forensic computer. He or she should also monitor any changes in the forensic computer caused by the tools.

Evidence-Collecting Tools and Equipment

The investigator should have general crime scene processing tools, such as the following:

- Cameras
- Notepads
- Sketchpads
- Evidence forms
- Crime scene tape
- Markers

The following are some of the tools and equipment used to collect the evidence:

- Documentation tools:
  - Cable tags
  - Indelible felt-tip markers
  - Stick-on labels
- Disassembly and removal tools:
  - Flat-head and Phillips-head screwdrivers
  - Hex-nut drivers
  - Needlenose pliers
  - Secure-bit drivers
  - Small tweezers
  - Specialized screwdrivers
  - Standard pliers
  - Star-type nut drivers
  - Wire cutters
- Package and transport supplies:
  - Antistatic bags
  - Antistatic bubble wrap
  - Cable ties
  - Evidence bags
  - Evidence tape
  - Packing materials
  - Sturdy boxes of various sizes
- Other tools:
  - Gloves
  - Hand truck
  - Magnifying glass
  - Printer paper
  - Seizure disk
  - Unused floppy disks
- Notebook computers:
  - Licensed software
  - Bootable CDs
  - External hard drives
  - Network cables

- Software tools:
  - DIBS Mobile Forensic Workstation
  - AccessData's Ultimate Toolkit
  - Teel Technologies SIM Tools
- Hardware tools:
  - Paraben forensic hardware
  - Digital Intelligence forensic hardware
  - Tableau Hardware Accelerator
  - WiebeTech forensic hardware tools
  - Logicube forensic hardware tools

First Response Basics

The following are some first response basics:

- Under no circumstances should anyone except qualified forensic analysts make any attempts to collect or recover data from any computer system or device that holds electronic information.
- Any information present inside the collected electronic devices is potential evidence and should be treated accordingly.
- Any attempts to recover data by untrained persons could either compromise the integrity of the files or result in the files being inadmissible in administrative or legal proceedings.
- The workplace or office must be secured and protected to maintain the integrity of the crime scene and the electronic storage media.

Incident Response: Different Situations

The first response to an incident may involve one of three different groups of people, each of which will have different tasks based on the circumstance of the incident. The three groups are as follows:

- System administrators
- Local managers or other nonforensic staff
- Laboratory forensic staff

First Response by System Administrators

The system administrator plays an important role in ensuring network protection and maintenance, as well as playing a vital role in the investigation.

Once a system administrator discovers an incident, it must be reported according to the current organizational incident reporting procedures. The system administrator should not touch the system unless directed to do so by either the incident/duty manager or one of the forensic analysts assigned to the case.

First Response by Nonforensic Staff

Nonforensic staff members are responsible for securing the crime scene and making sure that it is retained in a secure state until the forensic team advises otherwise. They should also make notes about the scene and those present to hand over to the attending forensic team. The surrounding area of the suspect computer should be secured, not just the computer itself.

First Response by Laboratory Forensic Staff

The first response by laboratory forensic staff involves the following six stages:

1. *Securing and evaluating the electronic crime scene*: This ensures that all personnel are removed from the crime scene area. At this point in the investigation, the states of any electronic devices are not altered.
   - Search warrant for search and seizure
   - Plan the search and seizure

- Conduct the initial search of the scene
- Health and safety issues

2. *Conducting preliminary interviews*: All personnel, subjects, or any others at the crime scene are identified. Their position at the time of entry and their reasons for being at the crime scene are recorded.

   - Ask questions
   - Check consent issues
   - Witness signatures
   - Initial interviews

3. *Documenting the electronic crime scene*: Documentation of the electronic crime scene is a continuous process during the investigation, creating a permanent record of the scene.

   - Photograph the scene
   - Sketch the scene

4. *Collecting and preserving the electronic evidence*: Electronic evidence is volatile in nature and easily broken, so particular precautions must be taken to prevent damage.

   - Collect evidence
   - Deal with powered-off or powered-on computers at the time of seizure
   - Seize portable computers
   - Preserve the electronic evidence

5. *Packaging the electronic evidence*: All evidence should be well documented, and all containers should be properly labeled and numbered.

6. *Transporting the electronic evidence*: Special precautions must be taken while transporting electronic evidence. Make sure that proper transportation procedures are followed to avoid physical damage.

   - Ensure proper handling and transportation to the forensic laboratory
   - Ensure the chain of custody is strictly followed

Securing and Evaluating the Electronic Crime Scene

The following checklist should be followed when securing and evaluating an electronic crime scene:

- Follow the policies of the legal authority for securing the crime scene.
- Verify the type of incident.
- Make sure that the scene is safe for the responders.
- Isolate other persons who are present at the scene.
- Locate and help the victim.
- Verify any data that is related to the offense.
- Transmit additional flash messages to other responding units.
- Request additional help at the scene if needed.
- Establish a security perimeter to see if the offenders are still present at the crime scene area.
- Protect evidence that is at risk of being easily lost.
- Protect perishable data such as pagers and caller ID boxes.
- Make sure that the devices that contain perishable data are secured, documented, and photographed.
- Find the telephone lines that are connected to devices such as modems and caller ID boxes.
- Document, disconnect, and label telephone lines and network cables.
- Observe the present situation at the scene and record observations.
- Protect physical evidence or hidden fingerprints that may be found on keyboards, mice, diskettes, and CDs.

Warrant for Search and Seizure

The investigating officer or first responder must perform the investigation process in a lawful manner, which means a search warrant is required for search and seizure. The following are the two types of relevant search warrants:

- *Electronic storage device search warrant*: This allows for search and seizure of computer components such as the following:
  - Hardware
  - Software
  - Storage devices
  - Documentation
- *Service provider search warrant*: If the crime is committed through the Internet, the first responder needs information about the victim's computer from the service provider. A service provider search warrant allows the first responder to get this information. The first responder can get the following information from the service provider:
  - Service records
  - Billing records
  - Subscriber information

Planning the Search and Seizure

A search and seizure plan should contain the following details:

- Description of the incident
- Incident manager
- Case name or title for the incident
- Location of the incident
- Applicable jurisdiction and relevant legislation
- Location of the equipment to be seized:
  - Structure's type and size
  - Where the computers are located
  - Who was present at the incident
  - Whether the location is potentially dangerous
- Details of what is to be seized (make, model, location, ID, etc.):
  - Types
  - Serial numbers
  - If the seized computers were running or powered down
  - Whether the computers were networked, and if so, what type of network, where data is stored on the network, where the backups are held, if the system administrator is cooperative, if it is necessary to take the server down, and the business impact of this action
- Other work to be performed at the scene (e.g., full search and evidence required)
- Search and seizure type (overt/covert)
- Local management involvement

Initial Search of the Scene

Once the forensic team has arrived at the scene and unloaded their equipment, they will move to the location of the incident and try to identify any evidence. A perpetrator may attempt to use a self-destruct program or reformat the storage media upon the arrival of the team. If a suspected perpetrator is using the system, an investigator should pull the power cord immediately.

An investigator should isolate the computer system (whether it is a workstation, a standalone, or network server) or other forms of media so that digital evidence will not be lost.

In many cases computer systems are backed up on a regular basis. If attackers erase files from the primary storage device, these files may still remain on the backup storage media.

Health and Safety Issues

In order to protect the staff and preserve evidence such as fingerprints, investigators should follow these health and safety precautions:

- All elements of an agency's health and safety plan should be clearly documented.
- Health and safety considerations should be followed at all stages of the investigation by everyone involved.
- The health and safety program should be frequently monitored and documented by designated agency representatives.
- All forensic teams should wear protective latex gloves for all search and seizure on-site operations.

Conducting Preliminary Interviews

Questions to Ask When a Client Calls the Forensic Investigator

When a client first calls the investigator, the investigator should ask the following questions:

- What happened?
- Who is the incident manager?
- What is the case name or title for the incident?
- What is the location of the incident?
- Under what jurisdiction are the case and seizure to be performed?
- What is to be seized (make, model, location, and ID)?
- What other work will need to be performed at the scene (e.g., full search and evidence required)?
- Is the search and seizure to be overt or covert, and will local management be informed?

Consent

A properly worded banner displayed at login and an acceptable-use policy informing users of monitoring activities and how any collected information will be used will satisfy the consent burden in the majority of cases.

There are instances when the user is present and consent from the user is required. It should never be taken as generally acceptable for system administrators to conduct unplanned and random monitoring activities.

In cases such as this, appropriate forms for the jurisdiction should be used and must be carried in the first responder toolkit. Monitoring activities should be a part of a well-documented procedure that is clearly detailed in the obtained consent.

Sample of Consent-To-Search Form

The first responder needs a search warrant for search and seizure of electronic evidence of the victim's computer, in addition to a voluntary consent-to-search form approved by a court of law for searching and seizing electronic devices and media. Figures 4-1 and 4-2 show examples of consent-to-search forms.

Witness Signatures

Depending on the legislation in the jurisdiction, a signature (or two) may or may not be required to certify collection of evidence. Typically one witness signature is required if it is the forensic analyst or law enforcement officer performing the seizure. Where two are required, guidance should be sought to determine who the second signatory should be.

CONSENT TO SEARCH ELECTRONIC MEDIA

I, _____, hereby authorize _____, who has identified himself / herself as a law enforcement officer, and any other person(s), including but not limited to a computer forensic examiner, he / she may designate to assist him / her, to remove, take possession of and / or conduct a complete search of the following: computer systems, electronic data storage devices, computer data storage diskettes, CD-ROMs, or any other electronic equipment capable of storing, retrieving, processing and / or accessing data.

The aforementioned equipment will be subject to data duplication / imaging and a forensic analysis for any data pertinent to the incident / criminal investigation.

I give this consent to search freely and voluntarily without fear, threat, coercion or promises of any kind and with full knowledge of my constitutional right to refuse to give my consent for the removal and / or search of the aforementioned equipment / data, which I hereby waive. I am also aware that if I wish to exercise this right of refusal at any time during the seizure and or search of the equipment / data, it will be respected.

This consent to search is given by me this _____ day of, _____

20_____, at _____ am / pm.

Location items taken from: _____

Consenter Signature: _____

Witness Signature: _____

Witness Signature: _____

Figure 4-1 This is an example of a consent-to-search form for electronic media.

The witness signature verifies that the information in the consent form and other written documents was correctly explained to, and supposedly understood by, the signatory or the signatory's legally authorized representative, and that informed consent was given freely.

Whoever signs as a witness must have a clear understanding of that role and may be called upon to provide a witness statement or attend court proceedings.

Conducting Preliminary Interviews

When preparing a case, computer forensic professionals (CFPs) start their investigation by collecting evidence and conducting preliminary interviews. As a part of their preliminary investigation, they talk to everyone present at the site at the time of the offense. After identifying the persons present at the time of the crime, the CFPs conduct individual interviews and note everyone's physical position and his or her reason for being there.

As part of the investigation process, the CFP first determines whether the suspect has committed a crime or has violated any departmental policies. Usually, departments establish certain policies regarding the usage of computers.

Adhering to departmental policies and applicable laws, the CFP gathers evidence and collects information from individuals, such as the following:

- Actual holders or users of any electronic devices present at the crime scene
- Usernames and Internet service providers
- Passwords required to access the system, software, or data
- Purpose of using the system

Form 1.1 Voluntary Consent to Search

Voluntary Consent to Search

I, _____, do hereby, freely, voluntarily and without threat, pressure or coercion of any kind, consent to a warrantless search of my

_____

_____ (Location and description of premises to be searched), by representatives of _____ (Police Department or Agency) and individuals in their company. These representatives are authorized by me to seize any items, materials or other property which they may deem to be of possible evidentiary value.

_____

Witness   Signature of person consenting to search

_____

Witness   Relationship to Premises being searched

DOB _____ SSN _____

Date _____ Time_____

Figure 4-2   This is an example of a voluntary consent-to-search form.

- Unique security schemes or destructive devices
- Any off-site data storage
- Hardware and software documents

If the evidence the CFP gathers suggests that the suspect has committed a crime, the evidence will be presented in court. If the evidence suggests that the suspect has breached company policy, the CFP will hand over the evidence at the corporate inquiry.

A CFP should keep the following points in mind during preliminary interviews:

- Identify all persons present.

- If the suspect is present at the time of the search and seizure, the incident manager or the laboratory manager may consider asking some questions. However, they must comply with the relevant human resources or legislative guidelines for their jurisdiction.

- During an initial interview suspects are often taken off guard, having been given little time to create a false story. This means that they will often answer questions such as, "What are the passwords for the account?" truthfully.

- If the system administrator is present at the time of the initial interview, he or she may help provide important information such as how many systems are involved, who is associated with a particular account, and what the relevant passwords are.

- A person having physical custody of evidence is responsible for the safety and security of that evidence.
- Whenever possible, evidence must be secured in such a way that only a person with complete authority is allowed access.

Typical questions could include the following:

- Are there any physical keys to the system?
- What are the users' IDs and passwords?
- What e-mail addresses are in use? What are the users' IDs and passwords for them?

Witness Statement Checklist

The checklist in Figure 4-3 shows the proper procedures for taking statements from witnesses.

Documenting the Electronic Crime Scene

Documentation of the electronic crime scene is a continuous process during the investigation that makes a permanent record of the scene. When documenting, an investigator should keep the following points in mind:

- It is essential to properly take note of the physical location and states of computers, digital storage media, and other electronic devices.
- Document the physical crime scene, noting the position of the mouse and the location of elements found near the system.
- Document details of any related or difficult-to-find electronic components.
- Record the state of computer systems, digital storage media, and electronic devices, including the power status of the computer.
- Take a photograph of the computer monitor's screen and note what was on the screen.
- The crime scene should be documented in detail and comprehensively at the time of the investigation.

Photographing the Scene

On arrival, the first step taken by the forensic team should be to photograph the scene. It is very important that this be done in a way that will not alter or damage the scene, and everything should be clearly visible.

The best course of action is to take various photographs of the crime scene. For example, an investigator should first take a photograph of the building and/or office number. This should be followed by an entry photograph (what is seen as one enters the crime scene) and then by a series of *360-degree photographs*. These are overlapping photographs depicting the entire crime scene. It is important to proceed all the way from the entire scene down to the smallest piece of evidence.

Crime scene photographs should be taken of the work area, including things such as computer disks, handwritten documents, and other components of the system. Photos should also be taken of the back of the computer system to accurately show how cables are linked. If this cannot be done on-site, then all cables must be labeled so the computer system can be reconnected at the forensic laboratory and photographed.

Sketching the Scene

After securing the scene, the CFP has to prepare a sketch of the crime scene. This sketch should include all details about the objects present and their locations within the office area. As with photographs, forensic professionals prepare many sketches of the complete scene, all the way down to smallest piece of evidence.

Collecting and Preserving Electronic Evidence

When an incident is reported in which a computer is thought to have played a part, that computer can incorrectly be the first and only item seized. The crime scene should be investigated in a way that covers the entire area, with the computer being at the middle of the circle.

ACTIONS	CHECK IF PERFORMED WELL
1. Sets the person at ease	
• explains reason for taking statement	___
• explains what may be required of witness	___
• explains the importance of telling the truth	___
• respects the legal rights of the individual being interviewed	___
2. Ensures the environment is appropriate to an interview	
• no unnecessary police officers present	___
• interviews one individual at a time	___
• demonstrates an understanding of the importance of establishing trust	___
• adapts procedures and techniques as appropriate in interviewing diverse victims/witnesses	___
3. Takes written statement when appropriate	
• asks witness to write or type	___
• writes or types the statement using the witness's own words	___
4. Asks the individual to provide a recorded statement when appropriate	
• ask the witness to make a statement under oath (if necessary)	___
• makes audio/video recording of the statement when possible	___
5. Is receptive to individuals offering information (active listening)	___
6. Attends to the individual's physical needs (e.g. food, drink and rest periods)	___
7. Keeps a record:	
• does not offer to keep information "off the record"	___
8. Obtains basic identifying data:	
• date (e.g. Saturday, 25th Sept. 1999)	___
• time started	___
• location	___
• name	___
• mailing address and residence	___
• date of birth	___
9. Differentiates between witness and warned statements	___
10. During interview:	
• listens effectively	___
• maintains momentum of dialogue	___
• patiently works to arrive at accurate information	___
• keeps statement sequential (if possible)	___
11. Uses questions for clarification and records answers	___
12. Has witness verify and correct the statement	___
13. Has witness sign the statement and witnesses the signature	___
14. Accurately and quickly transcribes oral statements	___

Figure 4-3 This is a typical witness statement checklist.

All collected evidence should be marked clearly so that it can be easily identified later. Pieces of evidence found at the crime scene should be first photographed, identified within documents, and then properly gathered. Markings on the evidence should, at the very least, include date and time of collection and the initials of the collecting person. Evidence should be identified, recorded, seized, bagged, and tagged on-site, with no attempts to determine contents or status.

Order of Volatility

Volatility is the measure of how perishable electronically stored data are. When collecting evidence, the order of collection should proceed from the most volatile to the least volatile. The following list is the order of volatility for a typical system, beginning with the most volatile:

1. Registers and cache
2. Routing table, process table, kernel statistics, and memory
3. Temporary file systems
4. Disks or other storage media
5. Remote logging and monitoring data that is related or significant to the system in question
6. Physical configuration and network topology
7. Archival media

Dealing with Powered-Off Computers

At this point in the investigation, an investigator should not change the state of any electronic devices or equipment. If it is switched off, the investigator should leave it off and take it into evidence.

Dealing with Powered-On Computers

When dealing with a powered-on computer, the investigator should stop and think before taking any action. The contents of RAM may contain vital information. For example, data that is encrypted on the hard disk may be unencrypted in RAM. Also, running process information is stored in RAM. All of this vital information will be lost when the computer is shut down or when the power supply is removed.

If a computer is switched on and the screen is viewable, the investigator should photograph the screen and document the running programs. If a computer is on and the monitor shows a screensaver, the investigator should move the mouse slowly without pressing any mouse button, and then photograph and document the programs.

Dealing with a Networked Computer

If the victim's computer is connected to the Internet, the first responder must follow this procedure in order to protect the evidence:

- Unplug the network cable from the router and modem in order to prevent further attacks.
- Do not use the computer for the evidence search because it may alter or change the integrity of existing evidence.
- Photograph all devices connected to the victim's computer, particularly the router and modem, from several angles. If any devices, such as a printer or scanner, are present near the computer, take photographs of those devices as well.
- If a screensaver is visible, move the mouse slowly.
- If the computer is on, take a photograph of the screen and document any running programs.
- Unplug all cords and devices connected to the computer and label them for later identification.
- Unplug the main power cord from the wall socket.
- Pack the collected electronic evidence properly and place it in a static-free bag.
- Keep the collected evidence away from magnets, high temperatures, radio transmitters, and other elements that may damage the integrity of the evidence.
- Document all steps involved in searching and seizing the victim's computer for later investigation.

Dealing with Open Files and Startup Files

When malware attacks a computer system, some files are created in the startup folder to run the malware program. The first responder can get vital information from these files by following this procedure:

- Open any recently created documents from the startup or system32 folder in Windows and the rc.local file in Linux.
- Document the date and time of the files.
- Examine the open files for sensitive data such as passwords or images.
- Search for unusual MAC (modified, accessed, or changed) times on vital folders and startup files.
- Use the dir command for Windows or the ls command for Linux to locate the actual access times on the files and folders.

Operating System Shutdown Procedure

It is important to shut down the system in a manner that will not damage the integrity of any files. Different operating systems have different shutdown procedures. Some operating systems can be shut down by simply unplugging the power cord from the wall socket, while others have a more elaborate shutdown procedure that must be followed, as detailed below:

- MS-DOS/Windows 3.*x*/Windows 9*x*, Windows NT, Windows XP, Windows Vista, Windows 7:
  - Take a photograph of the screen.
  - Document any running programs.
  - Unplug the power cord from the wall socket.
- UNIX/Linux:
  - Right-click on **Menu** and click **Console**.
  - If root user is logged in, enter the password and type sync;sync;halt to shut down the system.
  - If the root user is not logged in and the password is available, type su to switch to the root user, enter the password, and type sync;sync;halt to shut down the system.
  - If password is not available, unplug the power cord from the wall socket.
- Mac OS:
  - Record the time from the menu bar.
  - Click **Special** and then **Shut Down**.
  - Unplug the power cord from the wall socket.

Preserving Electronic Evidence

The following are the steps that should be taken to preserve electronic evidence:

- Document the actions and changes observed in the monitor, system, printer, and other electronic devices.
- Verify whether the monitor is on, off, or in sleep mode.
- Remove the power cable if the device is off. Do not turn the device on.
- Take a photo of the monitor screen if the device is on.
- Check dial-up, cable, ISDN, and DSL connections.
- Remove the power cord from the router or modem.
- Remove any floppy disks that are available at the scene to safeguard the potential evidence.
- Keep tape on drive slots and power connectors.
- Photograph the connections between the computer system and related cables, and label them individually.
- Label every connector and cable connected to peripheral devices.

For handheld devices:

- Personal digital assistants (PDAs), cell phones, and digital cameras store information in internal memory.
- Do not turn the device on if it is off.
- Leave the device on if it is already on.
- Photograph the screen display of the device.
- Label and collect all cables and transport them along with the device.
- Make sure that the device is charged.
- Collect additional storage media like Memory Sticks and CompactFlash cards.

Seizing Portable Computers

- Photograph the computer and connected equipment.
- Record which cables are connected to which ports.
- Photograph the connectors at the back of the computer and individually label them.
- Remove the battery.

Dealing with Switched-On Portable Computers

- Powered-on portable computers should be handled in the same way as a powered-on desktop PC.
- If a portable computer wakes up, the time and date this happens must be recorded.
- Prior to pulling the power cable on a portable computer, the battery must be removed.
- If it is not possible to remove the battery, pressing down on the power switch for 30 seconds will force the power off.

Packaging and Transporting Electronic Evidence

Evidence Bag Contents List

The panel on the front of evidence bags must, at the very least, contain the following details:

- Date and time of seizure
- Investigator who seized the evidence
- Names of the officers who took photographs or prepared a sketch
- Exhibit number
- Where the evidence was seized from
- Sites where individual items were found
- Names of the suspected persons
- A short summary of the details of the seizure
- Details of the contents of the evidence bag

Packaging Electronic Evidence

Investigators should keep these items in mind when packaging electronic evidence:

- Make sure the gathered electronic evidence is correctly documented, labeled, and listed before packaging.
- Pay special attention to hidden or trace evidence, and take the necessary actions to safeguard it.
- Pack magnetic media in antistatic packaging.
- Do not use materials such as plastic bags for packaging because they may produce static electricity.

- Avoid folding and scratching storage devices such as diskettes, CD-ROMs, and tapes.
- Make sure that all containers that contain evidence are labeled in the appropriate way.

Exhibit Numbering

All evidence collected should be marked as exhibits using this format:

aaa/ddmmyy/nnnn/zz

- *aaa* are the initials of the forensic analyst or law enforcement officer seizing the equipment
- *ddmmyy* is the date of the seizure
- *nnnn* is the sequential number of the exhibits seized by the analyst, starting with 001
- *zz* is the sequence number for parts of the same exhibit (for instance, *A* would be the computer, *B* would be the monitor, *C* would be the keyboard, etc.)

Transporting Electronic Evidence

When transporting electronic evidence, investigators should do the following:

- Avoid turning the computer upside down or putting it on its side during transportation.
- Keep the electronic evidence collected from the crime scene away from magnetic sources such as radio transmitters, speaker magnets, and heated seats.
- Store the evidence in a safe area away from high temperature and humidity.
- Avoid storing electronic evidence in vehicles for a long period of time.
- Avoid conditions of extreme heat, cold, or moisture because they can alter, change, or damage electronic evidence.
- Maintain the proper chain of custody on the evidence that is to be transported.

Storing Electronic Evidence

Electronic devices contain potential digital evidence such as system date, time, and configuration. This evidence may be lost due to improper and prolonged storage. Because digital and electronic evidence is fragile in nature, it can be altered or erased without a trace. While storing electronic evidence, the first responder should do the following:

- Ensure the electronic evidence is listed in accordance with departmental policies.
- Store the electronic evidence in a secure and weather-controlled environment.
- Protect the electronic evidence from magnetic fields, dust, vibrations, and other factors that may damage its integrity.

Chain of Custody

The CFP must follow the correct chain of custody when documenting a case. The chain of custody is a written description created by individuals who are responsible for the evidence from the beginning until the end of the case.

The chain of custody form is easy to use. The individual who takes ownership of a piece of evidence has the responsibility to safeguard and preserve it so that it can be later used for legal inquiry.

Chain of Custody Documentation

A chain of custody document contains the following information about the obtained evidence:

- Case number
- Name, title, address, and telephone number of the person from whom the evidence was received
- Location where obtained
- Reason for evidence being obtained
- Date/time evidence was obtained

- Item number/quantity/description
- Name of the evidence
- Color
- Manufacturing company name
- Marking information
- Packaging information

Simple Format of the Chain of Custody Document

Figure 4-4 shows the format of a chain of custody document.

Laboratory or Agency Name		Case Number:-	
Name and title from whom received		Address and telephone number	
Location from where evidence obtained		Reason of evidence obtained	Date/Time of evidence obtained
Item Number	Quantity	Description of Items	

Figure 4-4 This shows a typical format for a chain of custody document.

First Responder Common Mistakes

Often, when a computer crime incident occurs, the system or network administrator assumes the role of the first responder at the crime scene. The system or network administrator might not know the standard first responder procedure or have a complete knowledge of forensic investigation, so he or she might make the following common mistakes:

- Shutting down or rebooting the victim's computer. In this case, all volatile data is lost. The processes that are running on the victim's computer are also lost.

- Assuming that some components of the victim's computer may be reliable and usable. In this case, using some commands on the victim's computer may activate Trojans, malware, and time bombs that delete vital data.

- Not having access to baseline documentation about the victim's computer.

- Not documenting the data collection process.

Chapter Summary

- Electronic evidence is material of investigative value that is transferred by or stored on electronic devices.

- Health and safety issues are important in all of the work carried out in all phases of forensic procedures.

- Sometimes the user is present, and consent from the user is required.

- Documentation of an electronic crime scene is a continuous process during an investigation.

- The chain of custody is a written description created by individuals who are responsible for evidence from the beginning until the end of the case.

Review Questions

1. What is the chain of custody?

   _____

   _____

2. Describe the responsibilities of the first responder.

   _____

   _____

3. Describe the procedures for creating a first responder toolkit.

   _____

   _____

4. What information should be on the front of an evidence bag?

   _____

   _____

5. What are the different groups of people that might be involved in a first response?

   _____

   _____

6. Describe the order of volatility of electronic evidence.

_____

_____

7. Describe the format for exhibit numbering.

_____

_____

8. What information should be included in documentation concerning seized equipment?

_____

_____

Hands-On Projects

HANDS-ON PROJECTS

1. Read the DOE CFP First Response Manual.
   - Navigate to Chapter 4 of the Student Resource Center.
   - Open and read the document titled "DOE-CFL-FirstResponseManual.pdf."

2. Read First Responder.
   - Navigate to Chapter 4 of the Student Resource Center.
   - Open and read the document titled "First responder.pdf."

3. Read Forensics First Responder.
   - Navigate to Chapter 4 of the Student Resource Center.
   - Open and read the document titled "forensics_1st-responder.pdf."

4. Read the Responder Guide.
   - Navigate to Chapter 4 of the Student Resource Center.
   - Open and read the document titled "responder guide.pdf."

Chapter 5

Incident Handling

Objectives

After completing this chapter, you should be able to:

- Identify incidents
- Understand security incidents
- Report incidents
- Respond to incidents
- Handle incidents
- Understand CSIRTs
- Understand who works in a CSIRT
- Understand the types of incidents and levels of support
- Understand how a CSIRT handles a case
- Learn about CERTs all over the world

Key Terms

Social engineering a technique used to make a person reveal confidential information such as passwords through manipulation

Case Example

Orient Recruitment, Inc., is an online human resource recruitment firm. Jack, the network administrator, sees that the Web server is overloaded with connection requests from a huge number of different sources. Before he realizes that there is a serious attack underway, the Web site falls to the infamous denial-of-service (DoS) attack.

The company management contacts the local incident response team to look into the matter and solve the DoS issue. What steps will the team take to investigate the attack?

Introduction to Incident Handling

An incident is an event or set of events that threatens the security of computing systems and networks. It includes system crashes, packet flooding, and unauthorized use of another user's account. This chapter will show how these incidents are handled.

Types of Incidents

Incidents can be classified as one or more of the following:

- Repudiation
- Reconnaissance attack
- Harassment
- Extortion
- Pornography trafficking
- Organized crime activity
- Subversion
- Hoax
- Caveat

Repudiation

Repudiation is when a person or program, acting on behalf of another person, performs an invalid action.

Reconnaissance Attack

Collecting or discovering information about any individual or organization that might be useful in attacking that individual or organization is known as reconnaissance. DSL and cable modem connections are more exposed than others to reconnaissance attacks because the connections are usually open, which allows more time for attackers to attack the systems.

Port scanning, or running a program that remotely finds which ports are open or closed on remote systems, is one of the most common types of reconnaissance attacks.

Harassment

Harassing an individual using the Internet is a cyber crime in which the attacker sends a harassing message to a victim using e-mail, instant message, or any other form of online communication. Extreme cases of harassment include cyber stalking, in which electronic means are used to follow or intimidate the victim.

Extortion

An extortionist forces the victim to pay money to the attacker by threatening to reveal information that could lead to a severe loss for the victim. This loss could be data/information-related, or it could be a simple financial threat.

Pornography Trafficking

Using company computers for pornography is usually against company policy, and some forms of pornography are against the law. Computers and networks are being used extensively worldwide to store, send, and receive child pornography. Users embed pornographic images in other images, making it difficult to track the flow. One famous technology used for this purpose is steganography, discussed in a later chapter.

Organized Crime Activity

Some organized illegal activities, such as drug trafficking, illegal passport and visa creation, running prostitution rackets, and online smuggling, are done with the help of computers.

Subversion

Subversion is an incident in which a system does not behave in the expected manner. This leads the users to believe that this behavior is due to an attack on the integrity of the system, network, or application. In reality, it is something else entirely. An example of this would be placing a bogus financial server to discover credit card numbers or illegally index Web pages. In a subversive incident the perpetrator modifies the Web links so that whenever anyone uses one of the links, they are redirected to an unrelated Web address.

Hoax

A hoax is an e-mail warning of a virus that may have devastating effects on the system. The virus does not really exist, but a specific company is blamed for its imaginary effects, causing panic and unnecessary blame. The hoax convinces people to send e-mails to others, informing them about this supposed virus, panicking users who can then cause damage to their systems.

Caveat

A caveat is another type of warning, like a "Beware" sign posted near a dangerous area. It may be in the form of a legal notice that could lead to a court hearing. It may also just be a simple principle, as in *caveat emptor*. This means "buyer beware," as it is the buyer's job to check out the item before he or she pays for it.

Security Incidents

A security incident includes the following:

- Evidence of data tampering
- Unauthorized access or attempts at unauthorized access from internal and external sources
- Threats and attacks by an electronic medium
- Defaced Web pages
- Detection of some unusual activity, such as possibly malicious code or modified traffic patterns
- Denial-of-service attacks
- Other malicious attacks, such as virus attacks, that damage the servers or workstations
- Other types of incidents that weaken the trust and confidence in information technology systems

Categories of Incidents

Incidents can be classified as low-, mid-, or high-level incidents, depending on their intensity and effect.

Category of Incidents: Low Level

Low-level incidents are the least harmful incidents and should be handled within one working day. Low-level incidents could be any of the following:

- Compromise of a password
- Suspected sharing of an account
- Misuse of computer peripherals
- Unintentional routine computer action
- Unsuccessful scans and probes of the network
- Presence of computer virus or worm

Category of Incidents: Mid Level

Mid-level incidents are more serious kinds of incidents. They should be handled the same day the event occurs, and normally within two to four hours after the event has occurred. Mid-level incidents can be identified by observing any of the following:

- Unfriendly employee termination
- Violation of special or privileged access to a computer or any computing facility that would normally only be accessible to administrators

- Illegal access of the network
- Unauthorized storing or processing of data
- Destruction of property worth less than $100,000
- Personal theft of an amount less than $100,000
- Presence of computer virus or worm of higher intensity

Category of Incidents: High Level

High-level incidents are severe and should be handled as soon as possible. These include the following:

- Suspected computer break-in
- Denial-of-service attacks
- The presence of a harmful virus or worm, which can lead to serious corruption or loss of data
- Changes in hardware, software, and firmware without authentication
- Destruction of property worth more than $100,000
- Theft worth more than $100,000
- Child pornography
- Gambling
- Illegal downloads of copyrighted material, including music, videos, and software
- Other illegal file downloads
- Any violations of the law

Incident response teams handle high-level incidents. Such incident types are reported to the computer security officer.

Issues in Present Security Scenario

The Internet is growing at an extremely fast rate, with more and more companies venturing into e-commerce and more and more applications using the Internet. This not only means more traffic but also more complexity.

The reduction in product development cycles coupled with decreased testing cycles has caused an increase in software bugs. An unchecked vulnerability or a weakness in design could allow attackers to gain access.

The learning curve for carrying out network attacks is decreasing rapidly due to easily available hacking tools. In addition, the tools are more sophisticated, making them both more devastating and more difficult to stop.

Until recently, the need for an incident response team within every organization was never given serious thought. Since there is a lack of trained professionals, most organizations are opting for in-house incident response teams. This chapter highlights the need for an incident response team as well as the basic procedures for handling incidents.

How to Identify an Incident

Intrusion detection tools can warn the network administrator or staff about most security breaches much faster than manually identifying intrusions. The network administrator should be alert and check any suspicious activity on the network. Though an intrusion detection system (IDS) is important, relying on it does not ensure complete protection of the network and systems.

An administrator needs to watch for the following signs of security incidents:

- Suspicious log entries
- System alarms from the IDS
- Presence of unexplained user accounts on the network
- Presence of suspicious files or unknown file extensions on the system
- Modified files or folders

- Unusual services running or ports opened
- Unusual system behavior
- Changed drive icons
- Drives not accessible
- More packets received than expected

How to Prevent an Incident

The key to preventing incidents is minimizing vulnerabilities. This can be done using the following strategies:

- *Scanning*: Tools to monitor and scan for vulnerabilities should be placed throughout the network and used on a regular basis. Trained professionals should be on call to handle any discovered vulnerabilities.

- *Auditing*: Monitoring and compliance groups perform audits to ensure proper measures are taken when vulnerabilities are discovered.

- *Detecting intrusions*: Internet Security and Acceleration (ISA) Server logs should be reviewed, and remote-access audits performed to ensure that remote account access is enabled only for authentic users.

- *Establishing defense-in-depth*: The system administrator should establish a multilayered defense strategy, called defense-in-depth, rather than relying on a single point of protection.

- *Securing clients for remote users*: The system administrator should ensure that any users trying to remotely access the network are denied if they do not have correct patches, programs, and security settings.

Defining the Relationship Between Incident Response, Incident Handling, and Incident Management

Figure 5-1 illustrates the relationship between incident response, incident handling, and incident management. Incident response is one of the functions performed in incident handling. Incident handling is one of the services provided as part of incident management.

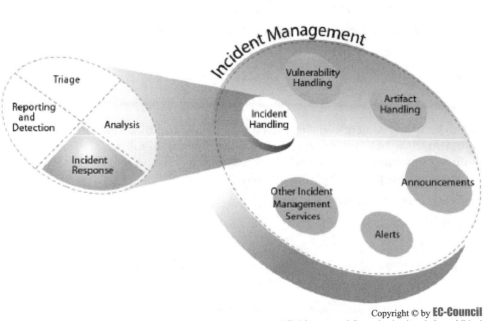

Figure 5-1 This shows how incident response, incident handling, and incident management are related.

Incident Management

Incident management involves not only responding to incidents but also triggering alerts to prevent potential risks and threats. Software that is open to attacks must be recognized before someone takes advantage of the vulnerabilities. Incident management includes the following:

- Vulnerability analysis
- Artifact analysis
- Security awareness training
- Intrusion detection
- Public or technology monitoring

Conducting training sessions to spread awareness among users is a part of incident management. This will help end users better recognize suspicious events or incidents with ease and to report an attacker's behavior to the appropriate authority.

Incident management activities are performed by the following people:

- *Human resources personnel* can take steps to fire employees suspected in harmful computer activities.
- *Legal counsel* set the rules and regulations in an organization. These rules can impact the internal security policies and practices of the organization when any system is used for harmful or malicious activities.
- The *firewall manager* keeps filters in place where denial-of-service attacks are made frequently.
- An *outsourced service provider* repairs systems infected by viruses and malware.

Threat Analysis and Assessment

Threat analysis is the systematic detection, identification, and evaluation of the vulnerabilities in a facility, operation, or system. It involves scrutinizing the conditions and processes that are important for preventing business interruption. Threat analysis is a key component in risk management decisions, while threat assessment examines each threat and its likelihood of occurrence.

The critical tasks of threat analysis and assessment include the following:

- Examining physical security processes
- Creating a risk management program
- Identifying and examining threats related to customers
- Providing data, trends, methodologies, and the likelihood of risk actions occurring
- Identifying and defining security process flows

Threat analysis involves both identifying risk and evaluating it.

Vulnerability Analysis

Vulnerability analysis or assessment is the process of identifying technical vulnerabilities present in computers and networks. It also identifies any weaknesses in system operation policies and practices. It is necessary to perform vulnerability analysis on all systems to safeguard critical data.

The vulnerability analysis process includes the following:

- Identification of present and potential threats
- Examining the threats
- Control measures
- Threat categorization based on severity, probability, and vulnerability
- Risk profile

The steps involved in vulnerability analysis are as follows:

1. Defining and classifying network or system resources
2. Assigning relative levels of importance to the resources
3. Identifying potential threats to each resource

4. Developing a plan to deal with the most serious potential problems

5. Defining and implementing ways to minimize the consequences if an attack occurs

Estimating the Cost of an Incident

Tangible losses can be quantified and include the following:

- Lost productivity hours
- Investigation and recovery efforts
- Loss of business
- Loss or theft of resources

Intangible losses, which are more difficult to identify and quantify, include the following:

- Corporate reputation
- Loss of goodwill
- Psychological damage, i.e., fear or loss of morale
- Legal liability

Change Control

Change control is a procedure that handles or controls all authorized changes to assets such as software and hardware. It also keeps track of access privileges and processes. It involves change requests, result recording, documenting, testing the results after the changes, and gaining approval for the requests.

Change control involves performing analysis of the problem, updating the results, and sending a request of the change to the concerned personnel or representative. This change is reviewed by the management, and if it is deemed necessary, authorization for the change is given.

Incident Reporting

A user encountering a breach should report the following:

- Intensity of the security breach
- Circumstances that revealed the vulnerability
- Shortcomings in the design, and impact or level of weakness
- Entry logs related to the intruder's activity
- Specific help needed, defined as clearly as possible
- Time of the breach, time zone of the region, and synchronization information of the system with a national time server via NTP (Network Time Protocol)

Computer Incident Reporting

Figure 5-2 shows a sample form for reporting an incident.

Where to Report an Incident

The incident should be reported to the CERT Coordination Center, site security manager, or other sites. It can also be reported to law enforcement agencies, such as the FBI and the USSS Electronic Crimes Branch if necessary. The incident should be reported in order to receive technical assistance and to raise security awareness in order to minimize losses.

Report a Privacy or Security Violation

In the event of a privacy or security violation, a user should report the following information:

- Date, time, and location of the incident
- What occurred
- How it occurred

```
┌──────────────────────────────────────────────────────────────────────────┐
│ STATUS                                                                     │
│   ☐ Site Under Attack        ☐ Past Incident    ☐ Repeated Incidents, unresolved │
│                                                                            │
│ CONTACT INFORMATION                                                        │
│ Name_____  Title_____  │
│ Organization_____ │
│ Direct-Dial Phone_____  E-mail_____   │
│ Legal Contact Name_____  Phone_____   │
│ Location/Site(s) Involved_____ │
│ Street Address_____ │
│ City_____  State_____  ZIP_____    │
│ Main Telephone_____  Fax_____   │
│ ISP Contact Information_____  │
│                                                                            │
│ INCIDENT DESCRIPTION                                                       │
│   ☐ Denial of Service            ☐ Misuse of Systems (internal or external) │
│   ☐ Distributed Denial of Service     (Includes inappropriate use by employees) │
│   ☐ Intrusion/Hack               ☐ Probe/Scan                              │
│   ☐ Malicious Code (virus, worm)  ☐ Unauthorized Electronic Monitoring (sniffers) │
│                                   ☐ Website Defacement                      │
│   ☐ Other (specify)_____  │
│                                                                            │
│ DATE/TIME OF INCIDENT DISCOVERY                                            │
│ Date_____  Time_____   │
│ Duration of Attack_____  │
│                                                                            │
│ IMPACT OF ATTACK                                                           │
│   ☐ Loss/Compromise of Data      ☐ System Downtime                         │
│   ☐ Damage to Systems            ☐ Other Organizations' Systems Affected   │
│   ☐ Financial Loss (estimated amount: $_____)               │
│   ☐ Damage to the Integrity or Delivery of Critical Goods, Services or Information │
│                                                                            │
│ SEVERITY OF ATTACK, INCLUDING FINANCIAL LOSS OR INFRASTRUCTURE             │
│  ☐ High       ☐ Medium       ☐ Low            ☐ Unknown                    │
│                                                                            │
│ SENSITIVITY OF DATA                                                        │
│  ☐ High       ☐ Medium       ☐ Low            ☐ Unknown                    │
│                                                                            │
│ How did you detect This?_____  │
│ Have you contacted law enforcement about this incident before? Who & when?_____ │
│ Has the incident been resolved? Explain_____   │
└──────────────────────────────────────────────────────────────────────────┘
```

Source: http://www.nitc.state.ne.us/. Accessed 2/2007.

Figure 5-2   This is a sample form for reporting incidents.

- Type of data affected in the violation (paper records, electronic records, or other data)
- Persons involved in the violation (names, titles, contact information, and their involvement)
- Any sudden damage known or observed
- Any corrective actions already taken

Preliminary Information Security Incident Reporting Form

Figure 5-3 shows a sample form for reporting a security incident.

Why Organizations Do Not Report Computer Crimes

All too often, computer crimes go unreported. Some of the reasons for this include the following:

- *Misunderstanding the scope of the problem*: Many organizations assume that their incident is unique and that no other company faces such attacks.
- *Fear of negative publicity*: Some may think that if word gets out about the attack, outsiders will think less of the company, thereby affecting its value. However, proactive reporting and handling will allow the company to put its own spin on the incident first, minimizing damage.
- *Potential loss of customers*

PRELIMINARY INFORMATION SECURITY INCIDENT REPORTING FORM
Background Information
Name of Bureau / Department :
Brief description on the affected system (e.g. function, URLs):

Physical location of the affected system:
    Within B/ D   Third-party service provider facility
System administration / operation by:
    In-house IT team   End user   Outsourced service provider

Reporting Entity Information
Name: Designation:
Office Contact: 24 hours Contact:
Email Address: Fax Number:
Incident Details
Date/ Time (Detected):   Date/ Time (Reported to OGCIO):
Symptoms of Incidents:

Impacts:
    Defacement of web site
    Service interruption (denial of service attack / mail bomb / system failure)
    Massive malicious code attack
    Lost/ damage/ unauthorized alternation of information
    Compromise/ leakage of sensitive information
    Intrusion / unauthorized access
    Others, please specify: _____
Please provide details on the impact and service interruption period, if any:

Actions Taken:
Current System Status:
Other Information:

Source: http://www.ogcio.gov.hk/. Accessed 2/2007.

Figure 5-3   This shows a sample form for reporting security incidents.

- *Desire to handle things internally*: It may be thought that the problem is small enough to be handled without outside help.
- *Lack of awareness of the attack*: Sometimes the attack just goes undetected, so the losses just go unexplained.

Incident Response

Response to a security incident is based on documented and uncorrupted evidence. The incident response procedure contains the following seven steps:

1. Identification of affected resources
2. Incident assessment
3. Assignment of event identity and severity level
4. Assignment of task force members
5. Containing threats
6. Evidence collection
7. Forensic analysis

Identification of Affected Resources

The incident investigator and coordinator (IIC) and the incident liaison (IL) work with the system personnel to determine the area and scope of an incident. This step is performed many times in the investigation process as more evidence and facts surface.

Incident Assessment

The IIC, in coordination with the IL and system personnel, perform the assessment process to determine the severity level. The IIC recommends further services for further assessment.

Assignment of Event Identity and Severity Level

In order to track and archive the incident for future reference, incidents should have a unique, collision-free identifier. The IIC assigns the identifier to the incident. A severity level is assigned to the incident after the identity assignment. The severity level determines the procedures and resources needed to successfully respond to and recover from an incident. Severity levels will be discussed later in this chapter.

Assignment of Incident Task Force Members

The IIC, supported by the IL, coordinates with the task force to resolve the incident. The task force consists of technical managers of resources, division managers, and other personnel. For level-one incidents, specific nondisclosure agreements must be signed (digitally or in person) by participants not directly involved in the incident response team. The IL distributes these agreements to the members involved in the task force at the initial stage of response coordination.

Containing Threats

Containment is required at the initial assessment of the incident. The IIC and the IL are responsible for determining the risks involved in the incident and the scope of the incident. When in need, remove the suspected resources to contain threats.

Evidence Collection

Information related to an incident is marked as evidence. The information is acquired from many sources, including: interviews with administrators, log files, unlinked files, exploit code left from an attacker, physical hardware, hard disk images, and kernel messages.

The evidence should consist of all the actions carried out on a computer or network. All evidence should include the following information:

- Tag number
- Description
- Time and date discovered
- Who has handled it

Notes about the incident should contain the data and a signature on each page. Electronic notes should contain a time stamp and be digitally signed.

Forensic Analysis

Evidence analysis should be done without any distraction in a secured and trusted environment. The examiner should analyze the evidence impartially and without any assumptions. The analysis should be documented, including the date and time of every action. If evidence must be moved, the examiner should keep a record of transport time, arrival time, and transport routing number of the evidence.

If a computer is seized, all of its components, including keyboard, mouse, network cables, and monitor, should also be seized. Incidents that involve intrusions will require the examiner to perform the analysis when the host is in a live state. Statically compiled utilities should be used during this form of analysis.

File analysis should be done against images of the media. Utilities used to make these images should not change the access, modification, or creation time of the media. The examiner should utilize cryptographic checksums to verify the copied media. Media involved in retaining the copies of the evidence must be sterilized. The evidence should be stored in a secure location.

Security Incident Response (Detailed Form)

The form shown in Figure 5-4 represents a detailed form for security incident response.

Incident Response Policy

A good incident response policy should include the following points:

- *Clearly outline management's support of the policy*: The policy should have management's support. It should be signed by a member of senior management or by someone with similar authority. The provisions of the incident response policy, such as financial resources, training to implement the policy, and countermeasures to violations, require management endorsement.

- *Decide on an organizational approach*: There are two common methods for handling an incident: contain, clean, and deny; or monitor and record. The method chosen is dependent on the final goal. If the goal is that of seeking prosecution or compensation, then it is very important to monitor the event

---

Contact Information and Incident

Last Name: _____   First Name: _____

Job Title: _____

Phone: _____   Alt Phone: _____

Mobile: _____   Pager: _____

Email: _____   Fax: _____

Incident Description

Date/Time and Recovery Information

Date/Time of First Attack: Date: _____   Time: _____

Date/Time of Attack Detected: Date: _____   Time: _____

Has the Attack Ended: Yes   No

Duration of Attack (in hours):

Severity of Attack: Low   Medium   High

Estimated Recovery Time of this Report (Clock)   _____

Estimated Recovery Time of this Report (Staff Hours)   _____

Estimated Damage Account as of this Report ($$$ Loss) _____

Number of Hosts Affected: _____

Number of Users Affected: _____

Type of Incident Detected:

Exposing Confidential/Classified/Unclassified Data	Theft of Information Technology Resources/Other Assets	Creating accounts	Altering DNS/Website/Data/Logs	Destroying Data
Anonymous FTP abuse	Attacking Attackers/Other Sites	Credit Card Fraud	Fraud	Unauthorized Use/Acess
Using Machine Illegally	Impersonation	Increasing Notoriety of Attacker	Installing Back Door/Trojan Horse	Attacking the Internet
ICQAbuse/IRC Abuse	Life Threatening Activity	Password Cracking	Sniffer	Don't Know

Other (Specify) _____
SB1386 – Is Email Notification Required?   Yes   No
SB1386 - Email Notification Sent Out?   Yes   No

Comments (Specify Incident Details and additional information):
_____

Figure 5-4   This is a detailed security incident response form.   *(continues)*

General Information

How Did You Initially Become Aware of the Incident?
Automated Software Notification
Automated Review of Log Files
Manual Review of Log Files
System Anomaly (i. e., Crashes, Slowness)
Third Party Notification
Don't Know
Other (Specify)

Attack Technique (Vulnerability Exploited / Exploit Used)
CVE/CERT VU or BugTraq Number
Virus, Trojan Horse, Worm, or Other Malicious Code
Denial of Service or Distributed Denial of Service Attack
Unauthorized Access to Affected Computer Privileged Compromise (Root/Admin Access) User Account
Compromise/Web Compromise (Defacement)
Scanning/Probing
Other

Suspected perpetrator(s) or possible motivation(s) of attack:
CSU staff/students/ faculty
Former staff/ students/faculty
External Party
Unknown
Other (Specify)

Malicious Code

Virus, Worm
Name or Description of Virus
_____

Is Anti-Virus Software Installed on the Affected Computer(s)?	Yes (Name)	No
Did the Anti-Virus Software Detect the Virus?	Yes	No
When was your Anti-Virus Software Last Updated?	_____	

Network Activity

Protocols
Name or Description of Virus
TCP   UDP   ICMP   IPSec   IP Multicast   Ipv6   Other
Please Identify Source Ports Involved in the Attack: _____
Please Identify Destination Ports Involved in the Attack: _____

Impact of Attack

Hosts
Individual Hosts
Does this Host represent an Attacking or Victim Host?   Victim   Attacker   Both
Host Name: IP Address:
Operating System Affected: Patch Level (if known):
Applications Affected: Database:
Others:
Primary Purpose of this Host:

User Desktop Machine	User Laptop Machine	Web Server
Mail Server	FTP Server	Domain Controller
Domain Name Server	Time Server	NFS/File System Server
Database Server	Application Server	Other Infrastructure Services

Bulk Hosts
Bulk Host Information (Details): _____
Comments (Please detail incident): _____

Data Compromised:
Did the attack result in a loss compromise of sensitive or personal information?   Yes   No   Other
Comments: _____
Did the attack result in damage to system(s) or date   Yes (Specify)   No   Other
Comments: _____

Law Enforcement:
Has Law Enforcement Been Notified?   Yes   No
Remediation:
Please detail what corrective actions have been taken (specify):
Comments: _____

Did Your Detection and Response Process and Procedures Work as Intended?
Comments: _____
Please provide Discovery Methods and Monitoring Procedures that would have Improved Your Ability to Detect an Intrusion.
Comments: _____

Are there Improvements to Procedures and Tools that would have Aided You in the Response Process
Comments: _____

Are there Improvements that would have Enhanced Your Ability to Contain an Intrusion
Comments: _____

Are there Correction Procedures that would have Improved Your Effectiveness in Recovering Your Systems
Comments: _____

Source: http://www.sjsu.edu/iso/docs/CSU_SecIncidentRespLongForm.doc. Accessed 2/2007.

Figure 5-4   This is a detailed security incident response form.

and record every aspect of the incident for later use as evidence in a court of law. If, on the other hand, the goal is to simply restore services as quickly as possible, then the approach should be to contain the damage, clean the malware, and deny the attacker further access.

- *Determine outside notification procedures*: If the policy is applied in a distributed event, then it is necessary to determine outside notification procedures. This includes to whom, when, and how they should be notified.

- *Address remote connections and encompass all remote employees or contractors*: The policy must include remote connections. It should include all contractors and employees, and it is necessary that it explain the necessity of disconnecting and removing user access during a security incident.

- *Define partner agreements*: Discuss the agreements with the service providers and customers, and define the right to monitor and disconnect the network if necessary.

- *Identify the members of the incident team and describe their roles, responsibilities, and functions*: Create an incident team and inform them of their responsibilities, roles, and working areas. The team should consist of experts in different areas, such as security and human resources.

- *Develop an internal communication plan that identifies who will be notified and how they will be contacted*: These plans help to avoid confusion during disasters. A well-defined communication plan helps create an efficient and coordinated response.

- *Define a method for reporting and historically archiving the incident*: With the help of this information, incidents can be prevented from recurring.

Computer Security Incident Response Team (CSIRT)

A computer security incident response team (CSIRT) is a service organization that is responsible for receiving, reviewing, and responding to computer security incident reports and activities. Their services are usually performed for a defined constituency. This constituency could be a parent entity such as a corporate, governmental, or educational organization; a region or country; a research network; or a paid client.

A CSIRT can be a formalized or an ad hoc team. A formalized team performs incident response work as its major job function. An ad hoc team is formed during an ongoing computer security incident or to respond to an incident when the need arises. In the United States, the most appropriate CSIRT would be US-CERT (United States Computer Emergency Readiness Team), under the Department of Homeland Security. This chapter will discuss CSIRTs in greater depth later.

Incident Response Checklist

Use the following checklist to be sure that the incident response is handled correctly:

- Verify incident
- Contact department/agency security staff
  - IT manager
  - Designee or others by department procedure
- Security designee contacts CSIRT member
  - Call or contact the appropriate CSIRT organization for your company, either for the state you are located in, the federal organization, or your individual company CSIRT
  - Be sure to inform the appropriate people in your organization, such as the office of the CIO or CSIO
- Isolate the systems, unless the CSIRT's decision is to leave the system connected to monitor an active attack
- Begin a log book (who, what, when, and where)
- Identify the type of incident (virus, worm, or hacker)
- Create a preliminary estimation of the extent of the problem, including the number of systems
- Contact the local police authority with jurisdiction at the location of the incident, coordinated with CSIRT
- Follow the server/operating system–specific procedures to snapshot the system

- Inoculate/restore the system
- Close the vulnerability and ensure that all patches have been installed
- Return to normal operations
- Prepare report and conduct follow-up analysis
- Revise prevention and screening procedures
- Log all actions

Response Handling Roles

The incident reported to an incident response or security team is subjected to an investigation. The IIC is a full-time member of the security team. A member of the incident response team acts as IL. The IL is selected by the IIC based on the area of impact of the incident.

Incident Investigator and Coordinator (IIC)

The incident investigator and coordinator (IIC) determines the severity level of the incident and performs investigative duties and technical analyses. Evidence collected at the time of investigation is to be supervised by the IIC, because in the event of prosecution, expert witness testimony is required.

The IIC, in combination with the IL, decides on how to recover from the specific incident. The IIC manages the evidence and life cycle of the incident, and protects the evidence for further use.

Incident Liaison (IL)

The incident liaison (IL) supports and coordinates with the IIC. The coordinated resources include the following:

- Hardware resources
- Personnel
- Emergency fund allocation

The IL acts as the secondary witness to all the changes made to the computer and network systems during forensic analysis. The IL should manage the documentation and reporting of all factual information and verify whether the documents are delivered to the correct executive-level personnel.

Senior System Manager (SSM)

The senior system manager (SSM) is responsible for controlling the access of various accounting modules and information. This involves maintaining user accounts, passwords, and physical keys. The tools utilized by the SSM will ensure data integrity, complete processing, and security management, while enabling users to work more productively. The SSM can allow software to run through a standard Web browser without client software. In short, the SSM is responsible for the security of the computer systems.

Information System Security Manager (ISSM)

The information system security manager (ISSM) is the person responsible for the establishment and maintenance of security required for risk management. The roles and responsibilities of the ISSM are as follows:

- Checks the level of security to manage risks
- Establishes the risk management process
- Ensures information resources for audit requirements and participation from all levels of employees to implement policies and procedures
- Prepares and maintains a disaster recovery plan for information resources

Information System Security Officer (ISSO)

Each team member reports information to the information system security officer (ISSO) for maintaining policies and procedures. The roles and responsibilities of the ISSO include the following:

- Identification of threats and vulnerabilities
- Identification of restricted, sensitive, and unrestricted information resources

- Developing and maintaining:
  - Risk management processes
  - Disaster recovery/contingency plan
  - Updated security procedures

Contingency Planning

The purpose of contingency planning is to maintain a backup for all documents in order to let the company or business function close to normally after an attack. The guidelines for contingency planning are as follows:

- *Starting point*: The starting point focuses on the development and maintenance of the contingency plan. This requires the whole team's involvement.
- *Impact analysis and risk assessment*: At this step, the team analyzes problems that can occur. It checks for the following three things and drafts them into a list for future reference:
  - What types of disasters can occur
  - The probabilities of their occurring
  - The severity of the problems
- *Developing the plan*: In this step, the contingency plan is structured and developed. The first step is to act upon the threat immediately. This requires emergency services, other specialists, or experienced personnel. It also sets the priority of what actions should be taken.
- *Testing the plan*: Once the plan is developed, it must be tested to determine whether it will actually work. The testing should be done by the personnel who would take charge of the plan in a real disaster. These testing results should be documented and recorded.
- *Personnel training*: Personnel need to undergo training to become familiar with the plan in order to perform their tasks and responsibilities effectively.
- *Maintaining the plan*: The plan should be updated as soon as a new process is added or deleted from the organization. This task should be assigned to particular personnel. If the process is changed, then it is necessary to change the plan and test it again.

The five major components of an IT contingency plan are as follows:

- *Supporting information*: Provides the introduction and detailed concept of the plan
- *Notification/activation*: Supplies the notification procedures and damage assessments, and offers activation of the plan
- *Recovery*: Provides information about recovering the data with the help of backups
- *Reconstitution*: Provides information about restoring the original site, testing systems to prevent further problems, and terminating operations
- *Plan appendices*: Provide the point-of-sale lists, system requirements, standard operating procedures, and vital records of the plan

Continuity-of-Operations Plan

A continuity-of-operations plan provides an alternative site to the organization for a period of up to one month to allow the organization to recover from a disaster and perform normal organizational operations. It is executed independently from the business continuity plan.

Budget/Resource Allocation

The two major roadblocks of an incident handling and response planning process are budget and resource constraints. In general, both budget and resources are allocated according to previous experiences and perceived risk. There is no standard rule or practice for budget allocation for this scenario because return of investment for incident handling in information systems cannot be measured. Documentation of previous incidents and losses may help decision makers to estimate the potential savings of preventing and handling an incident.

Incident Handling

Incident handling is a set of procedures performed to overcome various types of incidents caused by different vulnerabilities. Incident handling involves the following three basic functions:

- Incident reporting
- Incident analysis
- Incident response

Some of the benefits of incident handling include the following:

- It equips the organization with procedures that can be followed if incidents ever occur.
- It saves time and effort, which is otherwise wasted in fixing the damage caused by incidents.
- It helps the organization to learn lessons from past experiences and to recover from the losses.
- The skills and technologies required to tackle an incident can be determined in advance with the help of the incident reporting process.
- It protects the organization from the legal consequences that it may have to face in the case of a severe incident.
- It helps to determine similar patterns in incidents in order to handle them more efficiently.

Procedure for Handling Incidents

Whenever an incident is encountered, a certain set of procedures should be followed to keep track of the activities or events that occur. An analysis of the incident should be performed, including: to what extent the damage has occurred, what made the incident happen, and what security measures should be taken so that the same incident does not happen again.

In order to handle the incident, a particular standardized set of activities or steps should be taken. The incident response handling process consists of the following six stages:

1. Preparation
2. Identification
3. Containment
4. Eradication
5. Recovery
6. Follow-up

A list of personnel should be made so users can know who to contact, when to contact them, and how to contact them. The following pages will detail each of the steps, outlining what should and should not be done.

1. Preparation

Preparation makes the organization aware of potential damage to the security or integrity of a system by making the response plans familiar to the organization.

In every system on the LAN, only the administrator should be given full access. The staff members should be notified of regular changes with the help of bulletin boards and notices, and they should be familiarized with the latest kinds of viruses, worms, and spam.

Special tools should be used to avoid potential damage and threats from viruses and worms. The systems should always be updated with the newest antivirus software and eradication tools to ensure the safety of systems and the network.

Proper training should be provided to staff members so they are aware of the latest trends in security configuration and management. Periodic tests for incidents should be conducted to ensure everyone is ready at all times.

2. Identification

In the identification stage, an incident is analyzed to determine its nature, intensity, and effects on the network and systems. Staff members are provided with guidelines on how to identify an incident. They should take care to note the event properly in order to help the incident response team handle the situation.

Incidents are identified through the following four steps:

1. Validating the incident
2. Identifying the nature of the incident

3. Identifying and protecting the evidence

4. Logging and making a report of whatever anomalies have occurred

The following symptoms may indicate that an incident has occurred:

- An alarm generated by the IDS when it finds any anomaly in data packets sent across the network
- A person continuously tries to login unsuccessfully
- The presence of new files or folders on a system on the network, possibly due to a virus or worm
- Deletion of files or important data
- The administrator cannot make changes to files, open any file folders or directories, or start any service, possibly due to a denial-of-service attack
- Unusual system crashes

The nature of the incident should also be considered so that only the necessary actions are taken. Extra steps will waste valuable time.

The evidence must be preserved in a secure location and proper documentation should be maintained, indicating the sequence of individuals who handled the incident. The integrity of the evidence should be ensured by keeping it in tamper-proof media or by generating the cryptographic checksum or hash checksum. The date and time should also always be recorded.

A full backup of the system should be maintained. The attackers are aware that their evidence is being captured, so they tend to destroy every trace of data kept in the system.

3. Containment

Containment limits the extent and intensity of an incident. The first step taken in the containment stage deals with the critical information obtained during the identification stage. It is the job of the computer security officer (CSO) to investigate and discuss with management where to keep any sensitive data. The information should either be kept on a CD or any other system that may be disconnected from the network, or it should be passed on to another, safer network.

In some cases, if a simple or well-known virus is discovered that does not pose any severe threat, the organization should use virus eradication and detection tools and software to remove it.

The passwords on all affected systems, as well as any systems that interact with them, should be changed to minimize any further loss of data. The data on the systems must be backed up so that the other systems remain unaffected.

When a system's integrity or security is in question, it is inadvisable to log in as root on UNIX/Linux systems or as administrator on Windows-based systems. No commands should be typed, in order to keep the network safe.

If a network-based attack is detected, the staff members should be careful not to let the intruder know that they have detected the attack. The intruder might do more harm to other systems on the network by erasing every trace of the attack. Standard procedures, such as continuing to use intrusion detection systems and keeping antivirus software up to date, should be maintained.

4. Eradication

After the incident is identified and contained, the next step is to eradicate it. In the case of a virus, the incident response team should eliminate the virus from all systems and media, including flash drives and backup media, using approved virus eradication tools. There are various kinds of incidents that leave behind malicious objects that can be difficult to locate.

The data and information gathered during the containment phase will help in the termination and removal of any residual damage caused by the attack. They will also help to determine how the incident can be avoided in the future.

Protection tools and techniques such as firewalls, routers, and router filters should be used. A new system should be installed and pointed to a new IP address while the compromised system is taken offline. The team should use a vulnerability analysis tool to scan for any vulnerable systems used with the affected systems. This is necessary to find any weak areas in network designs in order to correct them.

5. Recovery

In this stage, the affected systems are restored to their normal states. This involves validating the systems and monitoring them for any further infection. This can only be done when the vulnerability has been completely removed.

First, the incident response team needs to determine the course of action. The intrusion can be simple or complex, depending upon the amount of damage or potential damage posed by the incident and will require an appropriate course of action depending on the type of intrusion and the systems involved.

Next, the team should monitor and validate the systems. The team members need to determine the integrity of the systems as well as that of any backups by attempting to read their data. After the data is recovered from the systems and backups, they are verified to check the success of the operation and to see if the system is back to normal task monitoring. This is done by checking the network loggers and system log files.

The system is then monitored for potential backdoors, which can result in a loss of data. Different incidents on different systems all have different response procedures.

6. Follow-Up

The process of following up on an incident as soon as the system recovers helps the incident response team effectively handle any similar incidents in the future. This is done through the following five steps:

1. *Performing a cost analysis*: A brief cost analysis should be done to determine the costs associated with the following:

   - Establishing an incident
   - Overcoming losses caused by the incident
   - Lost data
   - Losses in hardware and equipment

2. *Documenting incident cost*: The time required by the internal response team to respond to the incident and associated costs should be calculated. These costs include the following:

   - Associated monetary costs
   - Effect of the incident on the organization's business
   - Amount of data lost and costs associated with it
   - Any hardware loss

   Documentation is beneficial in determining both the financial costs associated with the incident as well as the necessary budget for future security efforts.

3. *Report preparation*: The incident response team is also responsible for the preparation of a report, including the lessons learned from the incident and the cost analysis described above. The reports obtained can be used for training staff and professionals. The report should specify ways to increase staff awareness without making any changes to security.

4. *Revision of policies and procedures*: Policies and procedures should be revised in accordance with changes in technology.

5. *Documenting the response quality of an incident*: The following questions should be asked:

   - Was the incident detected promptly and, if not, why?
   - Could different virus eradication and detection tools have helped?
   - Was there sufficient containment of the incident?
   - What particular difficulties were encountered?
   - Was there sufficient preparation for the incident?
   - Was the incident communicated properly?

Postincident Activity

It is important that the incident response team learn from every incident it encounters. The organization needs to host a meeting with all parties involved and ask the following questions:

- What type of incident took place?
- When did it take place?
- How well did the staff and management respond in combating the incident? Did they follow the documented procedures?
- What information was required?
- What should the staff do if a similar incident occurs?

- What preventive measures will prevent a similar incident in the future?
- What additional tools or resources are required to detect, analyze, and mitigate future incidents?

These meetings can also be helpful because the reports that they generate can be used as training material for new members. A follow-up report to be used in the future can be created for each incident.

Using Collected Incident Data

Data collected during the incident can be used for several purposes. Data such as total hours of involvement and the cost involved are used to secure additional funds needed for the incident response team. The data also help measure the success of the team. Incident data include the following:

- Number of incidents handled
- Time per incident
  - Total amount of labor hours working on the incident
  - Total time from the beginning to the end of an incident
  - Time taken for each stage of the incident-handling process
  - Time taken by the incident response team to respond to the initial report of the incident
- Objective assessment of each incident (determining the effectiveness of the response)
- Subjective assessment of each incident (performance evaluations)

Evidence Retention

Organizations should implement policies detailing the time that evidence for incidents should be retained. Factors to consider in making these policies include the following:

- *Prosecution*: If the attacker is prosecuted, then the evidence must be retained until legal actions are completed. Evidence that may seem insignificant at the time can be of importance in the future.
- *Data retention*: Organizations employ data retention policies that determine the time period for all data to be kept, regardless of whether an incident occurs.
- *Cost*: The cost to an organization increases when hard drives stored as evidence are kept for an extended period of time.

Education, Training, and Awareness

An education, training, and awareness program educates people on how to handle computer-related incidents. Education and training provide the skills required to implement incident handling policies. Training should be delivered to all teams regarding their roles, responsibilities, and specific tasks. Specific skills are needed to rebuild and recover from losses during the recovery process.

Practical training removes developmental errors, improves the effectiveness of procedures, and reduces the occurrence of miscommunication. Well-trained members can often prevent an incident or, at the very least, limit the resulting damage.

To conduct training programs, it is necessary that training materials be updated. A comprehensive training program for all employees is necessary after updating the plan. Conducting training and exercises ensures that first responders have the necessary level of preparedness and updated training materials.

Training should be conducted at specified intervals and include the following:

- Identification and operation of utility shutoff devices
- Location of emergency staging areas
- Basic first aid and survival techniques
- Emergency responsibilities and reassignment plans for all positions

Internal and external awareness campaigns are conducted for the following reasons:

- To generate awareness among all parties
- To encourage all parties to participate in the events

- To teach plan strategies
- To make arrangements before a disaster occurs

Postincident Report

Figure 5-5 shows a sample postincident report form.

Procedural and Technical Countermeasures

Procedural and technical countermeasures include media downgrade and declassification, destruction/sanitization of media, and emergency destruction.

<table>
<tr><td colspan="2">Post-Incident Report   Incident Ref. No.: _____</td></tr>
<tr><td colspan="2">Bureau/Department : _____</td></tr>
<tr><td colspan="2" align="center">Reporting Officer Details</td></tr>
<tr><td colspan="2">Report Date : _____</td></tr>
<tr><td colspan="2">Reported By
    Name   : _____
    Designation : _____
    Phone No. : _____
    Email Addr. : _____</td></tr>
<tr><td colspan="2" align="center">Incident Details</td></tr>
<tr><td colspan="2">Incident Date : _____</td></tr>
<tr><td colspan="2">Type of Incident:</td></tr>
<tr><td colspan="2">System Name and Description:</td></tr>
<tr><td colspan="2">Summary of Incident:</td></tr>
</table>

<table>
<tr><td>Event Sequence:
Date Time   Event</td></tr>
<tr><td>Action Taken and Result:</td></tr>
<tr><td>Current System Status:</td></tr>
<tr><td>Personnel Involved:
Name   Designation   Phone No.   Email Addr.   Role</td></tr>
<tr><td>Hacker Details (if any):</td></tr>
<tr><td>Computer Virus Details (if any):</td></tr>
<tr><td>Other Affected Sites/Systems:</td></tr>
<tr><td>Damage (including disruption/suspension of service):</td></tr>
<tr><td>Cost Factor (including loss caused by the incident and the recovery cost/manpower):</td></tr>
<tr><td>Recommended Action to Prevent Recurrence:</td></tr>
<tr><td>Other Comments:</td></tr>
<tr><td>Experience Learnt:</td></tr>
</table>

Source: http://www.ogcio.gov.hk/eng/prodev/download/g54_pub.pdf. Accessed 2/2007.

Figure 5-5   This is a sample postincident report form.

Media Downgrade and Declassification

Information is downgraded or declassified when the information is no longer considered sensitive. This can be due to the passage of time or the occurrence of a specific event. The process of declassification is not automatically an approval for public disclosure.

Destruction/Sanitization of Media

Once the media are destroyed, they cannot be recycled as originally intended. Physical destruction of media can be performed by using a variety of methods, with cross-cut shredding being the most common. Departments can destroy media on-site or through a third party that meets confidentiality standards.

Media sanitization is the process of deleting confidential data from storage media, with a reasonable guarantee that the data cannot be retrieved and reconstructed. If this is done incorrectly, data could be re-created by attackers or other unauthorized individuals. The sanitization process is especially important when storage media are transferred, become obsolete, are no longer usable, or are no longer required. It is difficult to recover deleted data from the media, but not impossible.

Emergency Destruction

Procedures should be in place for the emergency destruction of classified or sensitive information held in high-risk environments. When developing the plan, an incident response team member needs to consider the following:

- Volume, level, and sensitivity of the classified material
- Sensitivity of the operational assignment
- Potential for aggressive action

Vulnerability Resources

- *US-CERT Vulnerability Notes Database* (http://www.kb.cert.org/vuls/): Publishes information about a wide variety of vulnerabilities, including their technical descriptions, impact, solutions and workarounds, and lists of affected vendors
- *National Vulnerability Database* (http://nvd.nist.gov/): The U.S. government repository of standards based vulnerability management data, including databases of security checklists, security-related software flaws, misconfigurations, product names, and impact metrics
- *Common Vulnerabilities and Exposures List* (http://cve.mitre.org/): Free list of internationally known information security vulnerabilities and exposures

CSIRT

A computer security incident response team (CSIRT) is trained in dealing with security matters related to intrusions and incidents. The team secures networks from foreign attacks. It also trains employees about techniques to handle incidents and take necessary measures, as well as methods of reporting incidents. The incident response team must be present within an organization to ensure network security in that organization.

The CSIRT availability is 24/7. It provides a single point of contact for reporting security incidents.

CSIRT Vision

- The CSIRT must know its clients as well as possible.
- It should know its mission. What is its purpose and what will its job be?
- The team members should know the kind of incidents they are going to handle, what kind of activities will be performed, and what must be accomplished.
- They should also know the organizational structure. How do they operate? How is it tied together?
- They should know about the resources they have to facilitate their activities and duties. What funds are to be given by the organization's management for maintaining and implementing the CSIRT?
- The components of the CSIRT influence each other, between various IT teams and management.
- The CSIRT must record all information collected, especially if the team is spread over different places.

Motivation Behind CSIRTs

There has been an increase in the number of computer security incidents that are reported and in the number of organizations that are affected by these incidents. Organizations should be aware that security policies and practices are required as a part of their risk management strategies.

To protect information assets, new regulations should be applied. Systems and assets cannot be protected just by system and network administrators. A prepared plan and strategy is required.

Why an Organization Needs an Incident Response Team

Because security breaches are becoming more and more common, it is essential to take actions to stop them. The growth in the number of attackers and advancements in their hacking tools pose a great threat to security.

The CSIRT conducts expanded research programs about security concerns, which lead to advancements in the computer security of an organization. The team consists of technical specialists having high levels of skill in securing large and complex systems. The team members increase the awareness of ongoing issues related to cyber security, vulnerabilities, and threats.

Who Works in a CSIRT

CSIRT staff roles may include the following:

- Manager or team lead
- Assistant managers, supervisors, or group leaders
- Hotline, help desk, or triage staff
- Incident handlers
- Vulnerability handlers
- Artifact analysis staff
- Platform specialists
- Trainers
- Technology watch

Other roles may include the following:

- Support staff
- Network or system administrators
- CSIRT infrastructure staff
- Programmers or developers (to build CSIRT tools)
- Web developers and maintainers
- Media relations
- Legal or paralegal staff or liaisons
- Law enforcement staff or liaisons
- Auditors or quality assurance staff
- Marketing staff

Skills Needed in Staffing the Computer Security Incident Response Team

Personal Skills   CSIRT staff should possess the personal skills necessary to communicate with clients, team members, other response teams, a wide range of technical experts, and other individuals who may have various levels of technical understanding. The success and reputation of a CSIRT depends greatly upon the skills of its staff.

- *Communication*: CSIRT staff members are required to remain in communication to effectively determine what is happening, what facts are important, and what assistance is necessary, all without being condescending or talking above the comprehension level of the listener. This can be accomplished through:
  - Written communication
  - Oral communication

- *Presentation skills*: Skills are required for technical presentation, client briefings, panel discussions, and any other public speaking engagement. These knowledgeable staff members represent the CSIRT and often will need to explain its mission, goals, services, and strategic direction.

- *Diplomacy*: The CSIRT staff often is required to deal with organizations and individuals with different goals and specifications. Skilled CSIRT staff members have the ability to anticipate potential points of contention, respond appropriately, maintain good relations, and avoid offending others.

- *Ability to follow policies and procedures*: To ensure a consistent and reliable incident response service, CSIRT staff is expected to be ready to accept and follow all rules and guidelines. This is true even if the rules and guidelins are not well documented and regardless of whether the staff member personally agrees with them.

- *Team skills*: CSIRT staff members must be flexible in their work methods as productive and cordial team players. CSIRT staff members are required to be aware of their responsibilities, contribute to the goals of the team, and work together to share information and workload.

- *Integrity*: CSIRT staff must be trustworthy, discreet, and able to handle information in confidence according to the CSIRT guidelines, any client agreements or regulations, and/or any organizational policies and procedures. It is critical that staff members understand the distinction between their customer service role in providing support to their constituency and the requirement to ensure that information is secured and properly handled.

- *Knowing one's limits*: Individuals must recognize their limitations and take the help of the rest of the team, other experts, and management.

- *Coping with stress*: The CSIRT staff is required to cope with stressful situations ranging from an excessive workload, to an aggressive caller, to an incident in which human life or a critical infrastructure may be at risk.

- *Problem solving*: CSIRT staff is confronted with a significant amount of data every day. It is essential that the staff accomplish the following:

  - Determine the relevance of the data provided

  - Identify what information is important, missing, or might be misleading or incorrect

  - Decide how to handle that data

- *Time management*: To stay productive, CSIRT staff members are required to balance their efforts between completing assigned tasks, recognizing situations in which help or guidance from management should be sought, and avoiding situations that require constantly changing the priorities of assigned tasks.

Technical Skills

- *Technical foundation*: Staff must have a basic understanding of the underlying technologies used by the CSIRT and the client, as well as an understanding of issues that affect the team or client.

- *Incident handling*: Incident handling skills require an understanding of the techniques, decision-making strategies, and software tools required in the daily performance of CSIRT activities.

Team Models

Incident response teams are structured in one of the following three ways:

- Central incident response team
- Distributed incident response teams
- Coordinating team

Incident response teams can also use any of the following three staffing models:

- Employees
- Partially outsourced
- Fully outsourced

Delegation of Authority

Proper delegation of authority ensures an effective response to the incidents in accordance with the organization's response policy. The incident response team members should be given authority based on their skills, expertise, and experience.

Delegation of authority includes the following:

- *Allocation of tasks*: Duties are assigned to a team or an employee.
- *Empowerment*: After assigning the duties, a relevant authority will take control of the duties. The delegated authority is in charge of gathering materials and equipment, supporting other members, and providing information and advice without interfering in the task.
- *Responsibility*: Responsibilities include focusing on results and meeting deadlines.
- *Accountability*: The employees are accountable to their superiors for the satisfactory performance of their work. The management should give full credit to staff members for their success in the assigned work.

Categories of CSIRT Services

CSIRT services can be grouped into three categories:

- *Reactive services* are triggered by an event or request, such as a report of a compromised host, widespreading malicious code, software vulnerability, or an alarm from an intrusion detection or logging system. These services represent the majority of CSIRT work.
- *Proactive services* provide assistance and information to help prepare, protect, and secure client systems in anticipation of attacks, problems, or events. Performance of these services will directly reduce the number of incidents in the future.
- *Security quality management services* augment existing and well-established services that are independent of incident handling and are traditionally performed by other areas of an organization such as the IT, auditing, or training departments. If the CSIRT performs or assists with these services, the CSIRT's point of view and expertise can provide insight to help improve the overall security of the organization and identify risks, threats, and system weaknesses. These services are generally proactive but contribute indirectly to reducing the number of incidents.

All incidents managed by the CSIRT should be classified into one of the categories listed in Figure 5-6.

Incident Category	Sensitivity*	Description
Denial of service	S_3	• DOS or DDOS attack.
Forensics	S_1	• Any forensic work to be done by CSIRT.
Compromised Information	S_1	• Attempted or successful destruction, corruption, or disclosure of sensitive corporate information or Intellectual Property.
Compromised Asset	S_1, S_2	• Compromised host (root account, Trojan, rootkit), network device, application, user account. This includes malware-infected hosts where an attacker is actively controlling the host.
Unlawful activity	S_1	• Theft / Fraud / Human Safety / Child Porn. Computer-related incidents of a criminal nature, likely involving law enforcement, Global Investigations, or Loss Prevention.
Internal Hacking	S_1, S_2, S_3	• Reconnaissance or Suspicious activity originating from inside the Company corporate network, excluding malware.
External Hacking	S_1, S_2, S_3	• Reconnaissance or Suspicious Activity originating from outside the Company corporate network (partner network, Internet), excluding malware.
Malware	S_3	• A virus or worm typically affecting multiple corporate devices. This does not include compromised hosts that are being actively controlled by an attacker via a backdoor or Trojan. (See Compromised Asset)
Email	S_3	• Spoofed email, SPAM, and other email security-related events.
Consulting	S_1, S_2, S_3	• Security consulting unrelated to any confirmed incident.
Policy Violations	S_1, S_2, S_3	• Sharing offensive material, sharing/possession of copyright material. • Deliberate violation of Infosec policy. • Inappropriate use of corporate asset such as computer, network, or application. • Unauthorized escalation of privileges or deliberate attempt to subvert access controls.
* - Sensitivity will vary depending on circumstances. Guidelines are provided.		

Source: http://www.first.org/. Accessed 2/2007.

Figure 5-6   This table shows the categories of incidents.

Types of Incidents and Levels of Support

CSIRT's levels of support are based on the following:

- Type and severity of the incident or issue
- Type of client
- Size of the user community affected
- Available resources

Resources will be assigned according to the following priorities, beginning with the most important:

1. Threats to the physical safety of human beings
2. Root or system-level attacks on any machine
3. Compromise of restricted confidential service accounts or software installations, in particular those with access to confidential data
4. Denial-of-service attacks
5. Any of the above at other sites
6. Large-scale attacks of any kind, such as sniffing attacks, social-engineering attacks, password-cracking attacks, destructive virus outbursts, and attacks involving several machines or services; these types of attacks involve multiple reports from different reporting entities
7. Compromise of individual user accounts
8. Forgery and misreprcsentation, and other security-related violations of local rules and regulations

Types of incidents other than those mentioned will be prioritized according to their apparent severity and extent.

Service Description Attributes

For each service provided, the CSIRT should provide its client with service descriptions or formal service-level agreements in as much detail as possible. In particular, any service provided by the CSIRT should include an explanation of the attributes and descriptions as outlined in Figure 5-7.

Attribute	Description
Objective	Purpose and nature of the service.
Definition	Description of scope and depth of service.
Function Descriptions	Descriptions of individual functions within the service.
Availability	The conditions under which the service is available: to whom, when, and how.
Quality Assurance	Quality assurance parameters applicable for the service. Includes both setting and limiting of constituency expectations.
Interactions and Information Disclosure	The interactions between the CSIRT and parties affected by the service, such as the constituency, other teams, and the media. Includes setting information requirements for parties accessing the service, and defining the strategy with regard to the disclosure of information (both restricted and public).
Interfaces with Other Services	Define and specify the information flow exchange points between this service and other CSIRT services it interacts with.
Priority	The relative priorities of functions within the service, and of the service versus other CSIRT services.

Figure 5-7   This table shows the attributes of CSIRT services and their descriptions.

Incident-Specific Procedures

Virus and Worm Incidents

1. Isolate the system.
   - Isolate the infected system from the network.
   - Disconnect the server if a worm attack is suspected.
   - The CIO of the office gives authority to isolate the entire WAN from the outside world.
   - Log all actions.
2. Notify the appropriate authorities.
   - Notify CSIRT without delay.
   - Notify the departmental designated authority (IT manager or other designee).
   - CSIRT and the IT manager are accountable for notifying other personnel concerned.
3. Identify the problem.
   - Determine and isolate the suspected virus or worm-related files and processes.
   - Save a snapshot of the system before deleting any process from the system.
   - Each server/OS configuration has a separate, defined procedure for saving log files, history, and/or active processes.
   - Make a list of all active network connections.
   - Archive the infected files and then delete them.
   - Run the CSIRT recommended security software on the infected systems to find all modified system files, new programs, or hidden special files.
   - Log all actions.
4. Contain the virus or worm.
   - Delete any suspicious processes from the system.
   - Ensure that backups containing the virus or worm will not be used in the future.
   - If there is a worm attack, remember to keep the systems isolated from the outside world, cleaned up, and inoculated.
   - Log all actions.
5. Inoculate the systems.
   - Evaluate the intensity of the damage before applying the patches.
   - Apply patches to inoculate the systems from future attack.
   - Analyze the system to assess any damage caused by the intrusion.
   - If the offending code is not analyzed, use backup tapes to restore the system.
   - Apply patches after the system is restored in safe mode.
   - Log all actions.
6. Return to a normal operating mode.
   - Ensure that the systems are back to their original operational state and request that all users change their passwords.
   - Make sure that all infections are gone.
   - Log all actions.
7. Perform a follow-up analysis.
   - Perform a follow-up postmortem analysis after the system is restored to normal.
   - The follow-up analysis helps the CSIRT handle future security incidents.
   - Document the incident for reference.

- Evaluate the existing procedures if required.
- Eliminate all online copies of infected files, code, etc., from the systems.
- Provide recommendations to the management.
- Produce a security incident report.

Hacker Incidents

Hacker incidents include repeated login attempts, repeated FTP or telnet commands, and repeated dial-back attempts.

1. Identify the problem.
   - Identify the sources of the attacks by looking at system log files and active network connections.
   - Make copies of all audit trail information such as system log files and store them in a safe place.
   - Capture process status information in a file and then store that file in a safe place.
   - Log all actions.
2. Notify the appropriate authorities.
   - Inform the CSIRT and the IT manager within 30 minutes.
   - After consulting with the CSIRT, it may be necessary to notify the police with jurisdiction at the location of the attack.
   - If one of the CSIRT members cannot be reached, then the IT manager will have alternate procedures for notifying other levels of management.
3. Identify the hacker.
   - If the source of the attacks or the attacker can be identified, then the CSIRT (or a designated person) will contact the system administrator or security analyst for that site and attempt to obtain the identity of the hacker.
   - Log all actions.
4. Notify CERT.
   - If the source of the attacks cannot be identified, then the CSIRT will contact the Internet CERT and provide them with information concerning the attack.
   - Release of information must be approved by the office of the CIO, in conjunction with the heads of the departments involved.
   - Log all actions.
5. Perform a follow-up analysis.
   - After an incident has been fully handled and all systems are restored to a normal mode of operation, perform a postmortem analysis.
   - All involved parties (or a representative from each group) should meet to discuss actions that were taken and the lessons learned.
   - Evaluate and modify all existing procedures, if necessary.
   - All online copies of infected files, worm code, etc., should be removed from the systems.
   - A set of recommendations should be presented to the appropriate management levels.
   - A person designated by the incident coordination team should write an incident report and distribute it to the appropriate personnel.

Social Incidents

Responding to social incidents is somewhat different from responding to a worm or virus incident. Some attackers will use techniques to trick people into revealing passwords or other information that compromises a target system's security. These scams include telephoning a mark that has the needed information, and posing as a field service tech or a fellow employee with an urgent access problem. This type of hacking is generally referred to as *social engineering* and needs to be addressed as a real threat to the computing and communication

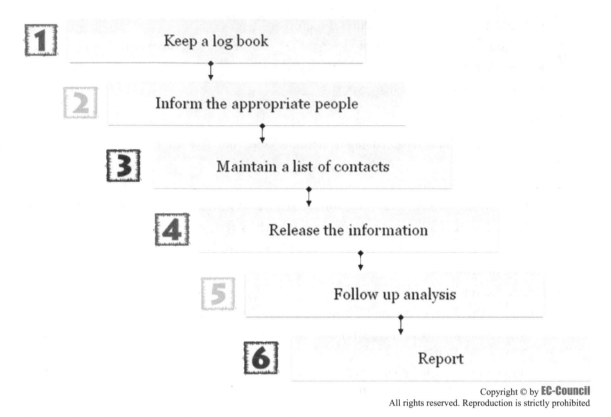

Figure 5-8   A CSIRT follows these steps in handling a case.

infrastructure. Once a hacker obtains an employee's password, the attacker will become more difficult to detect, and could cause damage and disruption.

An employee should notify a member of the CSIRT and the departmental security designee as soon as possible. The CSIRT will then be responsible for notifying other appropriate personnel. The team, with the help of the departmental technical staff, will be responsible for assessing what the attacker is attempting and the risks involved in letting the attacker continue. It may be necessary to contact the local authorities, depending on the location and activity of the attacker and the risks involved. As always, all actions should be logged.

Physical Incidents

It is essential to know how to respond to physical incidents on a daily basis. Any suspicious activity, such as unattended people wandering around or unlocked doors that are normally locked, could be a potential security risk.

Employees should confront individuals and ask for identification and the purpose of the visit. No one should make contact if he or she feels his or her safety is at risk.

If the incident is a physical intrusion, the employee should notify a member of the CSIRT and the departmental security designee as soon as possible. The CSIRT will then be responsible for notifying other appropriate personnel. Local authorities may be contacted depending on the location, suspicious activity, security breach, and risks involved. Again, all actions should be logged.

Steps a CSIRT Uses to Handle Cases

Figure 5-8 shows the steps a CSIRT uses in handling a case.

US-CERT Incident Reporting System

US-CERT is a partnership between the U.S. government, including the Department of Homeland Security, and the private sector. Established to protect the nation's Internet infrastructure, US-CERT coordinates defense

Section: Reporter's Contact Information

First Name *(Required)*	
Last Name *(Required)*	
Email Address *(Required)*	
Telephone number *(Required)*	
Are you reporting as part of an Information Sharing and Analysis Center (ISAC)?	No, this is not an ISAC report ▾
What type of organization is reporting this incident? *(Required)*	Please select ▾
What is the impact to the reporting organization? *(Required)*	Please select ▾
What type of followup action are you requesting at this time? *(Required)*	Please select ▾
Describe the current status or resolution of this incident. *(Required)*	Please select ▾
From what time zone are you making this report? *(Required)*	Please select a time zone ▾
What is the approx time the incident started? (localtime)	November ▾ 24 ▾ , 2008 ▾ : 05 ▾ : 55 ▾
When was this incident detected? (localtime)	November ▾ 24 ▾ , 2008 ▾ : 05 ▾ : 55 ▾

Section: Incident Details

Please provide a short description of the incident and impact *(Required)*

How many systems are impacted by this incident? (Leave blank if Unknown)	
How many sites are impacted by this incident? (Leave blank if Unknown)	
Was the data involved in this incident encrypted?	N/A ▾
Was critical infrastructure impacted by this incident?	N/A ▾
What was the primary method used to identify the incident	Unknown ▾

If available, please include 5-10 lines of time-stamped logs in plain ASCII text.(e.g.,CSV).

Source: http:/www.us-cert.gov/. Accessed 2/2007.

Figure 5-9   This is US-CERT's incident report form.

against and responses to cyber attacks across the nation. This system is used to report cyber-related incidents to US-CERT. The form shown in Figure 5-9 can be filled out at *http:/www.us-cert.gov/* to report incidents.

CSIRT Incident Report Form

Figure 5-10 shows a sample CSIRT incident report form, while Figure 5-11 shows a text-based incident report form.

Examples of CSIRTs

CSIRTs can be classified into the following types according to the services offered:

- Internal CSIRTs offer incident handling services to their parent organization, such as a bank, university, or federal agency.
- National CSIRTs provide services to the entire nation, such as Japan Computer Emergency Response Team Coordination Center (JPCERT/CC).

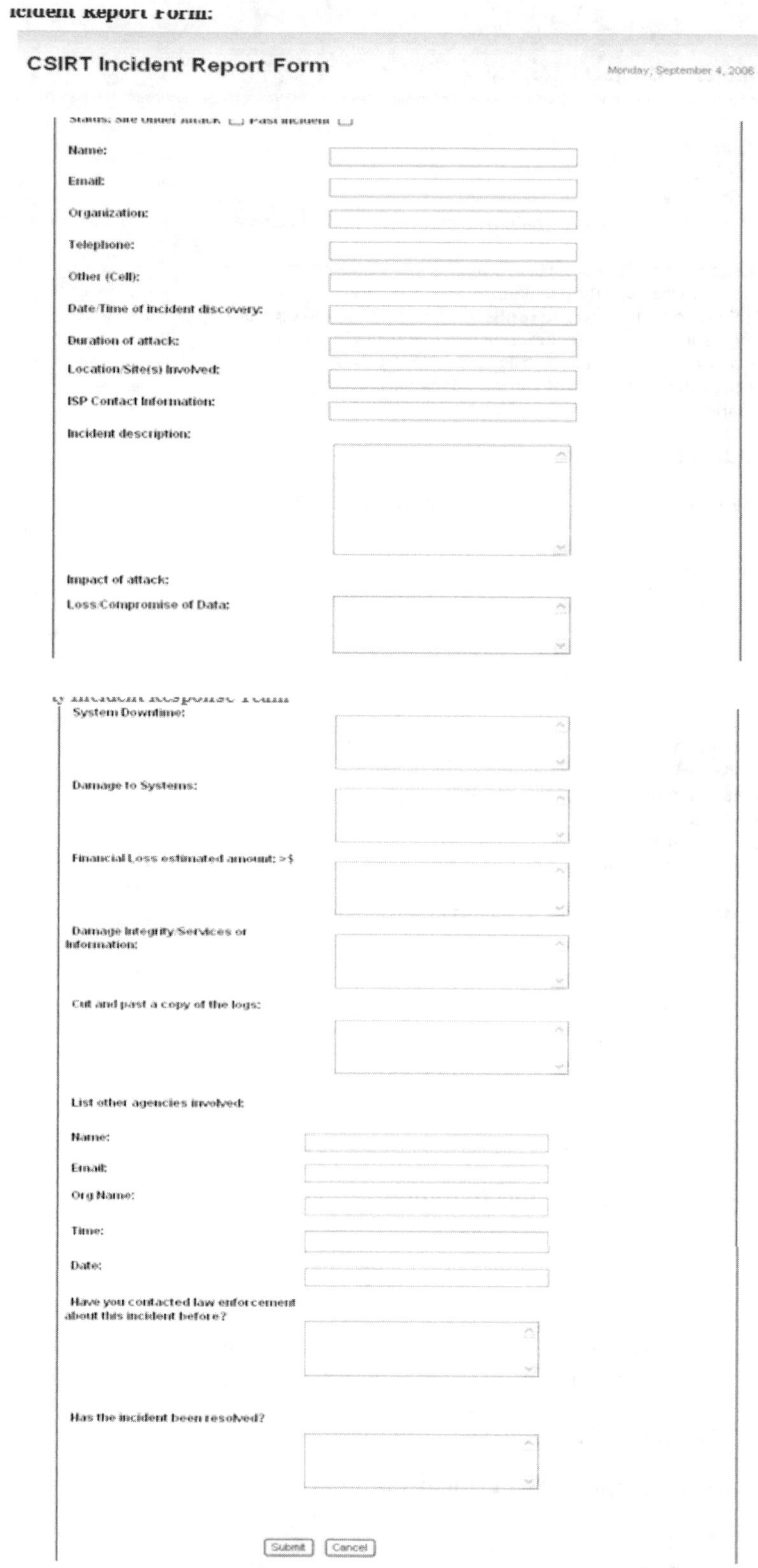

Icident Report Form:

CSIRT Incident Report Form

Status: Site Under Attack ☐ Past Incident ☐

Name:

Email:

Organization:

Telephone:

Other (Cell):

Date/Time of incident discovery:

Duration of attack:

Location/Site(s) Involved:

ISP Contact Information:

Incident description:

Impact of attack:

Loss/Compromise of Data:

System Downtime:

Damage to Systems:

Financial Loss estimated amount: > $

Damage Integrity/Services or Information:

Cut and past a copy of the logs:

List other agencies involved:

Name:

Email:

Org Name:

Time:

Date:

Have you contacted law enforcement about this incident before?

Has the incident been resolved?

[Submit] [Cancel]

Figure 5-10   This is a sample CSIRT incident report form.

```
Your contact and organizational information
1. name.....................:
2. organization name.........:
3. sector type (such as banking, education, energy or
     public safety)...........:
4. email address.............:
5. telephone number..........:
6. other.....................:

Affected Machine(s)
(duplicate for each host)
7. hostname and IP...........:
8. timezone..................:
9. purpose or function of the host (please be as specific
     as possible).............:

Source(s) of the Attack
(duplicate for each host)
10. hostname or IP...........:
11. timezone.................:
12. been in contact?.........:

13. Estimated cost of handling
      incident (if known).....:

14. Description of the incident (include dates, methods of
      intrusion, intruder tools involved, software versions
      and patch levels, intruder tool output, details of
      vulnerabilities exploited, source of attack, or any
      other relevant information):
```

Figure 5-11 This is a text-based CSIRT incident report form.

- Coordination centers can coordinate and facilitate the handling of incidents across various CSIRTs for a particular country, state, research network, or other entity.

- Analysis centers synthesize data from various sources to find trends and patterns in incident activities. This information is used to predict future activity or provide early warning when current activities match a set of previously determined characteristics.

- Vendor teams coordinate with organizations who report and track vulnerabilities. Other vendor teams provide internal incident handling services for their own organization.

- Incident response providers work for hire.

Steps for Creating a CSIRT

Step 1: Obtain Management's Support and Buy-In

Without management's approval and support, creating an effective incident response team can be difficult and problematic. Management's support can include the provision of resources, funding, and time. The participation and the input of executive and business or department managers and their staffs are essential in the design process.

It is important to fulfill the management's expectations as well as the CSIRT's function and responsibilities. A lack of this information can result in a team with unstructured services and authority.

In addition to management support for the planning and implementation procedure, management must commit to uphold CSIRT operations and authority for the long term.

Step 2: Determine the CSIRT Development Strategic Plan

The CSIRT can prove to be a failure if not managed properly. Various issues, including the following, need to be solved during this stage:

- Are there specific time frames to be met? Are they realistic, and if not, can they be changed?
- Is there a project group? Where do the group members come from? Ensure that all stakeholders are represented. Some may not be on the team for the whole project but are brought in to provide subject matter expertise and input as needed. If anyone has a background in project management, organizational behavior theory, and communications theory, consider having him or her participate on the team.
- How is the organization informed about the development of the CSIRT? A memo sent from the CIO, CEO, or other high-level manager announcing the project and asking each key stakeholder and area to provide assistance in any way possible is a good way to start. Informing the organization of the plan for the CSIRT in the early stages of development can help staff members feel they are part of the design process.
- If there is a project team, how is information collected and communicated, especially if the team is geographically dispersed?

Step 3: Gather Relevant Information

CSIRT is futile if it is unable to understand the organization's requirements for incident response. This not only includes what services to offer but also whether the CSIRT team is skilled enough to handle specific situations. This information can be collected through general discussions or interviews with key stakeholders, including the following:

- Business managers
- Representatives from IT
- Representatives from the legal department
- Representatives from human resources
- Representatives from public relations
- Any existing security groups, including physical security
- Audit and risk management specialists
- General representatives

Determine if anyone else is providing the same kinds of services offered by the CSIRT. If so, find out if those services can move to the CSIRT over the course of an agreed-upon period of time. Dealing with such issues can help identify what responsibilities are to be outlined and what information is to be gathered. Resources available for reviewing the gathered information include the following:

- Organization charts for the enterprise and specific business functions
- Topologies for organizational or constituency systems and networks
- Critical system and asset inventories
- Existing disaster recovery or business continuity plans
- Existing guidelines for notifying the organization of a physical security breach
- Any existing incident response plans
- Any parental or institutional regulations
- Any existing security policies and procedures

Step 4: Design the CSIRT Vision

The main focus in designing the CSIRT vision is to clearly communicate what is expected from the CSIRT. The vision for the CSIRT must give a clear description of how the CSIRT functions match with the current organizational structure and how the CSIRT intermingles with its clients. The vision explains what benefits the CSIRT provides, what processes it enacts, who it coordinates with, and how it performs its response activities.

- Identify the constituency. Who does the CSIRT support?
- Define the CSIRT's mission, goals, and objectives. What does the CSIRT do for the identified constituency?

- Select the CSIRT services to provide. How does the CSIRT support its mission?
- Determine the organizational model. How is the CSIRT structured and organized?
- Identify required resources. What staff, equipment, and infrastructure are needed to operate the CSIRT?
- Determine sources of funding. How are the initial startup as well as the long-term maintenance and growth of the CSIRT funded?

Step 5: Communicate the CSIRT Vision

The next step in the strategy is to communicate the CSIRT vision and operational plan to management, the constituency, and others who need to know and understand its operations. Make amendments to the plan based on any input given by them.

Communicating the vision beforehand can not only make the implementation process easier, it can assist in determining organizational problems before implementation. This kind of approach can let people know the development of the plan and permit them to give feedback regarding it. This is a way to begin marketing the CSIRT to the constituency and to gain the needed support from all organizational levels.

This process also helps in gaining information that may have been missed during the information-gathering process. This information and input can contribute to making final adjustments to the CSIRT's organizational structure and processes.

Step 6: Begin CSIRT Implementation

Implementation of the CSIRT commences as soon as the management's support and funding are obtained. It may include the following:

- Hiring and training initial CSIRT staff
- Buying equipment
- Building any necessary network infrastructure to support the team
- Developing the initial set of CSIRT policies and procedures to support its services
- Defining specifications and building the incident tracking system
- Developing incident reporting guidelines and forms

Incident reporting guidelines define how the constituency interacts with the CSIRT, what constitutes an incident, what types of incidents to report, who should report an incident, why an incident should be reported, the process for reporting an incident, and the process for responding to an incident. These guidelines should be clear and easy to understand.

There must be a detailed description of the various ways an incident can be reported, whether by phone, e-mail, Web form, or some other mechanism. It should also include details about what type of information should be included in the report.

The CSIRT strategy to prioritize and handle received reports should be communicated. This includes how the person reporting an incident is notified of its resolution, any response time frames that must be followed, and any other notification that occurs.

Step 7: Announce the CSIRT

When the CSIRT is operational, broadly announce it to the constituency or parent organization. It is best if this announcement comes from sponsoring management. Include the contact information and hours of operation for the CSIRT as well as the incident reporting guidelines. A simple flyer or brochure outlining the CSIRT mission and services, which can be distributed with the announcement, may help. Some teams have held an open house or special celebration to announce the operational CSIRT.

Once the CSIRT is operational, the effectiveness of the team can be evaluated. These evaluation results can be used to improve CSIRT processes and ensure the team's capability in meeting expectations. Information on effectiveness can be gathered through a variety of feedback mechanisms, including the following:

- Benchmarking against other CSIRTs
- General discussions with constituency representatives
- Evaluation surveys distributed to constituency members on a periodic basis
- Creation of a set of criteria or quality parameters that is then used by an auditing or third-party group to evaluate the team

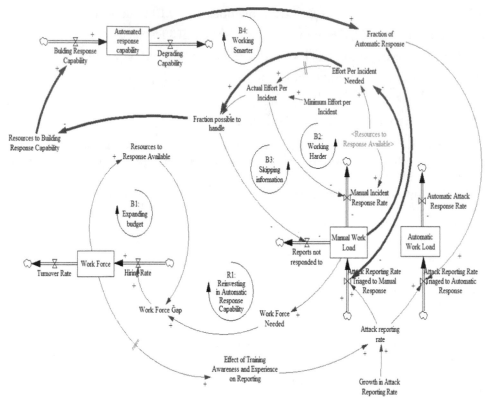

Source: http://www.cert.org/archive/pdf/Limits-to-CSIRT-Effectiveness.pdf. Accessed 2/2007.

Figure 5-12   Automation can increase the efficiency of a CSIRT.

Limits to Effectiveness in CSIRTs

A fundamental problem for a CSIRT is to balance a growing workload with limited human resources. A CSIRT can work smarter by investing in automation. When a problem is well understood, it becomes easier to solve. This is typically accomplished by altering some of the policies in the system or by reengineering parts of it.

Figure 5-12 shows how automated responses can increase effectiveness.

World CERTs

- *APCERT (Asia Pacific Computer Emergency Response Team)*: APCERT is an alliance of CSIRTs from 13 nations across the Asia Pacific region. Its first conference was held in March 2002 in Tokyo, Japan. A general meeting called APSIRC is organized annually. Any CSIRT from the Asia Pacific region will be permitted to be a member of APCERT after meeting all member accreditation requirements. APCERT members can be either full or general members.

- *AusCERT (Australia Computer Emergency Response Team)*: AusCERT from Australia is one of the leading CERTs in the Asia Pacific region. Its major objectives are providing computer incident prevention, response and mitigation strategies for members, a national alerting service, and an incident reporting scheme.

- *HKCERT (Hong Kong Computer Emergency Response Team Coordination Center)*: HKCERT was established to deal with security threats and cyber crimes. It regularly organizes awareness seminars and training courses on information security–related topics. Its objective is to provide a centralized contact for computer and network security incident reporting and response. It coordinates the response and recovery actions for all reports. It offers guidance for monitoring and disseminating information on security-related issues and advises preventive measures against security threats.

- *JPCERT/CC (Japan Computer Emergency Response Team/Coordination Center)*: JPCERT/CC is an independent nonprofit organization established in 1992. It acts as a central association in Japan to deal with computer-related and network security–related issues. It gathers computer incident and vulnerability information, and issues security alerts and advisories. It provides education and training to increase awareness of security issues.

- *MyCERT (Malaysian Computer Emergency Response Team)*: MyCERT was introduced on January 13, 1997, and began operation on March 1, 1997, from the Mimos Berhad office at the Bukit Jalil Technology Park Malaysia. It suggests countermeasures for computer security incidents and methods of prevention to the Internet community.

- *PakCERT (Pakistan Computer Emergency Response Team)*: PakCERT was formed to deal with security services and to guard against attackers. Its aim is to impart education, technology, and experience while maintaining the highest level of secrecy in the industry. It strengthens network and computer security with up-to-date tools.

- *SingCERT (Singapore Computer Emergency Response Team)*: SingCERT was initially established in October 1997 in collaboration with the Center for Internet Research, National University of Singapore (NUS). It is a program of the Infocomm Development Authority of Singapore (IDA) and is responsible for security incident response in Singapore.

- *TWCERT/CC (Taiwan Computer Emergency Response Team/Coordination Center)*: TWCERT/CC is a one-stop center for computer-related or Internet-related incident response teams in Taiwan. Its major objective is to handle computer security incidents and vulnerabilities, uniting system-related and network-related resources to prevent potential problems and improve security.

- *CNCERT/CC (China Computer Emergency Response Team/Coordination Center)*: CNCERT/CC was introduced in October 2000 as a functional organization under the Internet Emergency Response Coordination Office of the Ministry of Information Industry of China. It became a member of FIRST (Forum of Incident Response and Security Teams) in August 2002 and took an active part in the establishment of APCERT. It is responsible for the coordination of actions of all computer emergency response teams inside China concerning incidents in national public networks. Its main objectives are providing computer network security services and technology support in all security incidents for national public networks, important national application systems, and key organizations, including detection, prediction, response, and prevention. It assembles, validates, accumulates, and publishes authoritative information on Internet security issues and is also responsible for the exchange of information and coordination of action with international security organizations.

North American CERTs

- *CERT-CC (Computer Emergency Response Team/Coordination Center)*: CERT-CC is located at the Software Engineering Institute (SEI), a federally funded research and development center at Carnegie Mellon University in Pittsburgh, Pennsylvania. It was established with the joint efforts of the Defense Advanced Research Projects Agency (DARPA) and SEI. Its main objectives upon being established were to provide response to major security incidents and to analyze product vulnerabilities. In modern days its responsibilities have been expanded to stay abreast of advanced intruder techniques, increased amounts of damage, increased difficulty of detecting an attack, and increased difficulty in catching attackers. Currently it is a part of the SEI network systems survivability program, whose goal is to guarantee suitable technology and system management practices that are used to protect networks from attacks, minimize damages, and ensure the continuity of the critical services in spite of successful attacks, accidents, or failures.

- *US-CERT (The United States Computer Emergency Readiness Team)*: US-CERT was formed in 2003 to protect the nation's Internet infrastructure. It is a partnership between the U.S. government, including the Department of Homeland Security, and the private sector. Throughout the nation, US-CERT manages defense against and responses to cyber attacks. Its main objectives are analyzing and reducing cyber threats and vulnerabilities, disseminating cyber-threat warning information, and coordinating incident response activities. It interacts with federal agencies, the tech industry, the research community, state and local governments, and others to disseminate reasoned and actionable cyber-security information to the public.

- *CanCERT (Canadian Computer Emergency Response Team)*: CanCERT was Canada's first national Computer Emergency Response Team, established in 1998 by EWA-Canada Ltd. Operating 24/7, its main objective is to be the trusted center for the collection and dissemination of information related to networked computer threats, vulnerabilities, incidents, and incident response for the Canadian government, as well as business and academic organizations.

- *FIRST (Forum of Incident Response and Security Teams)*: Since 1990, FIRST has resolved security-related attacks and incidents, and handled thousands of security vulnerabilities. FIRST collects a wide variety of security and incident response teams, especially product security teams, combining the government, commercial, and academic sectors.

South American CERTs

- *CAIS [The National Education and Research Network (Rede Nacional de Ensino e Pesquisa – RNP)]*: CAIS is the Brazilian network of all federal institutions of higher education and research. It provides a test platform for the experimental development of new applications and network services.

- *NBS/CAIS—Brazilian Research Network CSIRT/NIC BR Security Office Brazilian CERT*: NBS/CAIS—Brazilian Research Network CSIRT/NIC BR Security Office Brazilian CERT is the Brazilian computer emergency response team, sponsored by the Brazilian Internet Steering Committee. This team is responsible for receiving, evaluating, and taking action on computer security incident reports on the Brazilian Internet.

European CERTs

- *EuroCERT (European CERT)*: EuroCERT was founded on September 15, 1999. It is a part of the SIRCE (Security Incident Response Coordination for Europe) pilot, which is sponsored by TERENA and provides support, coordination, and information for CSIRTs in Europe.

- *Funet (Finnish University and Research Network)*: Funet is a network service center for scientific computing, providing services to universities, polytechnic colleges, and other research communities. It was formed with the help of the Finnish Ministry of Education. The main objective of Funet is to help its member organizations enhance computer and network security.

- *SURFnet-CERT (Computer Emergency Response Team of Netherlands)*: SURFnet-CERT is an Internet provider to higher-education institutes and various other research institutes in the Netherlands. This team was previously known as CERT-NL. SURFnet-CERT deals with all cases related to computer security incidents in which a SURFnet customer is involved, either as a victim or as a suspect. SURFnet-CERT also provides security-related information to SURFnet customers on a structural basis (e.g., distributing security advisories), or on an incidental basis (e.g., distributing information during emergencies).

- *DFN-CERT (Deutsche Forschungsnetz CERT)*: DFN-CERT, established on November 13, 2001, is a level-two team according to the CERT rules of the Trusted Introducer.

- *JANET-CERT*: JANET-CERT is a UK computer response team provided by UKERNA. It also provides services to customers under contract with HEANet. This team also publishes advice for security awareness and methods to improve security and networks. It delivers training courses, discusses other events related to computer security, and works with other worldwide, European, and UK CERT organizations to provide a security information base for its customers.

- *CERT POLSKA (CERT NASK/Research and Academic Network in Poland)*: CERT POLSKA was known as CERT NASK prior to 2001. It has been a full member of the worldwide Forum of Incident Response and Security Teams since 1997. The current CERT POLSKA headquarters are located at the NASK site in Warsaw, Poland. Its main objective is to provide a reliable, trusted single point of contact in Poland for the NASK community and their respective networks to prevent and deal with network security incidents. It also provides security information warnings about possible attacks on other corporations around the world.

- *Swiss Academic and Research Network CERT*: The Swiss Confederation funds this institution, protecting SWITCH (Swiss Research Group), the member organizations of SWITCH, and their networks.

Chapter Summary

- A computer security incident is defined as any real or suspected undesirable event in relation to the security of computer systems or computer networks.
- Handling incidents involves three basic functions: incident reporting, incident analysis, and incident response.
- Incident reporting is the process of reporting information regarding an encountered security breach in the proper format.
- A CSIRT provides rapid response to maintain the security and integrity of systems.
- Building an effective incident response capability is difficult without management's support and approval.

Review Questions

1. How is an incident identified?

2. What are the procedures for handling an incident?

3. Describe five different types of incidents.

4. What is the difference between a mid-level incident and a high-level incident?

5. Describe the reasons that some organizations don't report computer-related incidents.

6. What is change control?

7. Describe the steps involved in creating a CSIRT.

8. Describe three examples of CSIRTs.

Hands-On Projects

1. Visit the vulnerability database at Securiteam.

   ■ Go to *http://www.securiteam.com/*.

   ■ View the vulnerability listings.

2. Visit the Zone-h database for hacking attempts.

   ■ Go to *http://www.zone-h.org/*.

   ■ Click the **Attack Archives** link.

   ■ View the defaced Web pages.

3. Read documents on incident handling.

   ■ Navigate to Chapter 5 of the Student Resource Center.

   ■ Read the document titled "csirt-handbook.pdf."

   ■ Read the document titled "Creating-and-Managing-CSIRTs-notes.pdf."

Chapter 6

Investigative Reports

Objectives

After completing this chapter, you should be able to:

- Understand the need for an investigative report
- Understand report specifications
- Understand report classification
- Describe the layout of an investigative report
- Understand the guidelines for writing a report
- Use supporting material
- Understand the importance of consistency
- Understand the salient features of a good report
- Understand the investigative report format
- Know the elements of a sample forensic report
- Understand the best practices for investigators
- Write a report using FTK

Key Terms

Testimonial evidence   oral evidence, presented by a competent eyewitness to the incident, that is relevant and material to the case

Introduction to Investigative Reports

An investigative report is a report that provides detailed information on the complete forensic investigation process. Computer forensic investigators collect all of the information involved in a case, investigate and analyze the information, and prepare a final investigative report. This report contains the results of the forensic investigation.

The following are the exhibits relevant to the computer forensic report:

- Photographs or diagrams
- Curriculum vitae of witnesses

The following are some of the elements of an investigative report:

- Should contain a description of how the incident occurred
- Should be technically sound and understandable
- Should be properly formatted, and there should be page and paragraph numbers for easy referencing
- Should contain unambiguous conclusions, opinions, and recommendations, supported by figures and facts
- Should adhere to local laws to be admissible in court

This chapter focuses on investigative reports. The remainder of this chapter describes the various elements of an investigative report. It also discusses the format of an investigative report and how to write a good report.

Investigative Report Template

The following is a sample investigative report template:

- Summary:
  - Case number
  - Names and Social Security numbers of authors, investigators, and examiners
  - Purpose of investigation
  - Significant findings
  - Signature analysis
- Objectives
- Date and time the incident allegedly occurred
- Date and time the incident was reported to the agency's personnel
- Name of the person or persons reporting the incident
- Date and time the investigation was assigned
- Nature of claim and information provided to the investigators
- Location of the evidence
- List of the collected evidence
- Collection of the evidence
- Preservation of the evidence
- Initial evaluation of the evidence
- Investigative techniques
- Analysis of the computer evidence
- Relevant findings
- Supporting expert opinion
- Other supporting details:
  - Attacker's methodology
  - User's applications
  - Internet activity
  - Recommendations

Report Specifications

In today's digital world, reports are generally submitted electronically to the court. The standard format for reports is Portable Document Format (PDF). Reports should be filed through an attorney. Filing reports directly with the court should be avoided.

Since a report is written for an investigation, it should showcase the mission or goal of the investigation. The motive is to find information on a specific subject, recover significant documents, or recover certain file types with a date and time stamp. The client, who can be an investigator or attorney, should define the goal of the investigation.

As much as possible, a report should be written in a logical order. The report should be written in such a way that it states the problem, presents the results of the investigation, and sets forth the conclusions and recommendations.

Report Classification

Report writing should begin with the identification of the audience and the objective of the particular report. The investigative report should be presented in such a manner that a person with lesser technical knowledge is also able to understand the findings and proceedings of the case.

Reports can be categorized as the following:

- Verbal
- Written

These categories are further divided into the following:

- Formal
- Informal

Verbal Formal Report

A verbal formal report is generally delivered to a board of directors, to managers, or to a jury. An attorney should prepare a document called an examination plan. This document contains expected questions and relevant answers, and it guides the investigator. An investigator can propose changes, such as those involving clarification or definition, to the attorney if an expression or term is misused. The investigator should not include things that are not related to the testimony.

Verbal Informal Report

Generally, a verbal informal report is less structured than a formal report and is submitted to a person within the attorney's office. This report is a preliminary report and should not be mishandled or inadvertently released. It mentions the areas of investigation yet to be completed, such as tests that may not have been concluded, interrogations, document production, and depositions.

Written Formal Report

A written formal report is a report sworn under oath, such as an affidavit or declaration. It is essential to pay attention to word usage, grammar, spelling, and details while writing formal reports. Due to the formal nature of this type of report, the first-person voice is preferred. For formal report writing, an investigator should use natural language.

Written Informal Report

A written informal report is a report that precedes the main events of a particular case. These reports are high-risk documents that contain sensitive information that could prove beneficial for the opposing counsel. The opposing counsel may receive the document in discovery. Discovery is an attempt made to obtain documents before a trial. This may be a written request for admissions of fact, depositions, or questions and answers written under oath.

It is advisable to include the contents of a written informal report in an informal verbal report. The investigator should summarize things such as subject system, tools used, and findings in the verbal informal report. Investigators should not destroy the written informal report if produced; this act is considered destruction or concealment of evidence, which in legal terms is known as *spoliation*.

Layout of an Investigative Report

While writing reports, an investigator should pay attention to the layout and presentation aspects of the report. It is advisable to adhere to one layout while writing a report, to maintain consistency.

The most important part of any investigative report is language. To communicate the information clearly, an investigator should include signposts. A signpost serves as a guide to readers; it draws their attention to a point or to the sequence of a process. For example, within the sections, the steps could be introduced with "The first step in this section" or "The second step in the examination." In this example, "first" and "second" are the signposts for the sequence of information.

Investigators should avoid superfluous statements such as "The following report is submitted" or "As the result of the investigation, I have to report as follows." Usage of proper format, style, tone, punctuation, vocabulary, and grammar is a must while writing a report.

There are two methods for numbering a report:

1. Decimal numbering structure
2. Legal-sequential numbering structure

Decimal Numbering Structure

The decimal numbering structure divides the text into sections. By viewing this structure, readers can easily go to the headings of the report. It also helps the reader to know how the textual parts are related to each other.

The following is an example of the decimal numbering structure:

1.0 Introduction
    1.1 Nature of incident
    1.1.1 Victim
2.0 First Incident
    2.1 Witness
        2.1.1 Witness testimony
3.0 Location of Evidence
    3.1 Seizure of evidence
        3.1.1 Transportation of evidence
4.0 Analysis of Evidence
    4.1 Chain of evidence
        4.1.1 Extraction of data
5.0 Conclusion
    5.1 Results
        5.1.1 Expert opinion

Legal-Sequential Numbering Structure

It is used in pleading legal cases and is popular among lawyers. Roman numerals stand for major aspects of the report and Arabic numerals for supporting information. The following is an example of the legal-sequential numbering structure:

I. Introduction
    1. Nature of the incident
    2. The victim
    3. Witnesses to the crime
    4. Location of the evidence
II. Examination
    1. Chain of evidence
    2. Extraction of evidence
    3. Analysis of evidence

Guidelines for Writing a Report

The following are some guidelines for writing a report:

- Write opinions that are based on knowledge and experience.
- Create a logical structure from beginning to end.
- Try to avoid hypothetical questions.
- Apply theoretical questions to guide and support opinions based on the factual evidence.
- Avoid using repetitive and vague language.
- Use a simple format so the report can be easily passed from one person to another.
- Group associated ideas and sentences into paragraphs and later into sections.
- Do not use slang words, specialist language (which is not understood by the average person), and colloquial terms (which creates the effect of conversation).
- If any abbreviations or acronyms are used, define and explain them in detail.
- After completing the report, check the grammar, vocabulary, punctuation, and spelling.
- Always use the active voice when writing a report so that the communication looks direct and straightforward.
- Write the report in a concise manner so that it is easily understandable and interesting to any audience.
- Write everything with proper validation.
- Never mention any clues in the report.
- Avoid writing many details and personal observations in the report.

Use of Supporting Material

A well-written investigative report tells a story that answers various questions relating to who, what, when, where, why, and how. Supporting materials such as figures, tables, data, and equations help the story unfold in an effective manner.

The investigator can reference the supporting material directly in the text. The points that the supporting material makes are integrated into the writing to enhance the impact. It is advisable to number figures and tables in the same order as they are introduced in the report. For example, tables can be numbered as Table 1, Table 2, and so on. Numbering the material avoids confusion and makes it easier to understand.

Full-sentence captions are preferred, rather than simple titles as captions. If charts are used, they should be labeled, including axes and units. Tables and figures should be inserted after the paragraph in which they are discussed.

Importance of Consistency

The following are some of the sections an investigative report should include:

- Abstract or summary
- Table of contents
- Body of report
- Conclusions
- References
- Glossary
- Acknowledgments

The sections can be adjusted to suit the purpose of the report.

An abstract or summary is meant to provide the essence of a report in an informative way. An abstract is an abbreviated or condensed form of the investigation that presents the main ideas. A table of contents should be designed to provide quick reference to important features of the investigation. The main points highlight the purpose of the report. References and appendices list the materials referred to during report writing. Any format can be followed for presentation.

It is not necessary to follow this exact format, but maintaining consistency is a must. For example, investigators should follow a consistent style of headings and subheadings throughout. Establishing a template can make it easier to maintain consistency.

Salient Features of a Good Report

A good report should have the following features:

- *Method explanations*: The investigator should provide a detailed explanation of how the problem was approached. Examination procedures, materials or equipment used, analytical or statistical techniques, and data collection of sources are a few subsections that can be included to make the reader understand the investigation process.

- *Data collection*: The data collection process is a critical factor, so it is important to present data in a well-organized format. While preparing the lab report, the investigator should record data such as observations in a laboratory notebook. All the tables used for presenting data should be labeled.

- *Calculations*: It is advisable to include all calculations that are done during the investigation in a summarized form. The investigator should provide the common name of any calculations that have one. The investigator should also provide a brief description of the standard tools and sources used for calculations.

- *Uncertainty and error analysis*: An investigator needs to provide a statement of uncertainty and error analysis during observation. During a computer investigation, it is necessary to provide the limitations of knowledge to protect integrity. For example, if a time stamp for a certain file is retrieved from a computer, the investigator should state explicitly that a time stamp can be reset easily, so the time stamp is not necessarily reliable.

- *Results explanations*: The investigator should explain all results in a logical order, using subheadings with text addressing the purpose of the report. The investigator should use tables and figures within the writing to enhance the presentation. Presentation of the results should be in such a way that any reader, whether he or she has knowledge of the case or not, can understand the whole investigation process based solely on the investigative report.

- *Discussion of results and conclusions*: Discussing results and conclusions is a must. The investigator should reframe all findings in light of an overall examination. The investigator should establish the significance of the research in this section. He or she should answer questions pertaining to how the case developed, what the problems were, and how the problems were approached.

- *References*: The investigator should organize the references in a standard format. Sufficient detail should be provided to allow another person to track down and verify the information. This section should list books, journal articles, leaflets, Web sites, and other materials referred to in the report. The investigator should also cite all quotes, paraphrases, or summarizations of another person's opinions.

- *Appendices*: Appendices contain extra material that is referred to in the report. Appendices include charts, diagrams, graphs, transcripts, and copies of materials. In addition to the pertinent figures, a brief description of each item and a reference to exhibits containing the documents supporting each item can be included. The investigator should arrange appendices in the same order as they are referred to in the report. Some portions of the appendices may be optional, and some may be required. For example, exhibits are required.

- *Acknowledgments*: An acknowledgment is not a dedication, but generally thanks people who helped during the research. For example, some people may have contributed to the analysis, and some people may have helped by proofreading. Acknowledgments are optional.

Important Aspects of a Good Report

The following are some of the important aspects of a good report:

- It is designed to help the judiciary come to a conclusion regarding the case.

- A good report shows the answer for each and every question that may be raised during a judicial trial.

- Facts and findings must be based on the evidence so that the judiciary can rely on the conclusions of the report.

- The report is written in an easy and neutral language so that every reader and decision maker understands it clearly.
- The report should convey all necessary information in a concise manner.
- The report should be structured in a logical manner so that information can be easily located.
- It should be written carefully and reviewed critically and thoroughly.
- It should contain tables, summary exhibits, footnotes, and appendices to reduce the narrative and present the findings in an interesting and readable format.

Investigative Report Format

Each firm, such as a law firm or a computer forensic firm, has its own established report format. An investigator can follow a previously written sample when writing a new report.

Before writing the report, the investigator should review the facts to determine which to include and which to exclude from the report. The investigator should carefully examine the information to ensure it is relevant to the case. The report must include all relevant evidence, even evidence that does not support the conclusion. It is essential for the investigator to project objectivity in the report and document the findings in an impartial and accurate manner.

An investigative report format basically has four sections:

Section 1 is the administrative section listing the investigating officials, how to contact them, and where the working papers are located.

Section 2 is dedicated to the background and summary. It includes a summary of the complainant's allegations, optional information that may help the reader understand the case, the outcome of the case, and the list of allegations.

Section 3 is reserved for the introduction of the first allegation. It presents the facts, analyzes and discusses the facts, and, if appropriate, makes a recommendation. A conclusion can be stated in this section, and it can also include documentation concerning the corrective action that a responsible authority took regarding any substantiated allegations. Any other allegations should be addressed in the same way. More sections can be introduced depending on the number of allegations.

Section 4 (or the last section) lists and describes the interviewees, the documents reviewed, and any other evidence gathered.

Attachments and Appendices

Attachments and appendices help maintain the flow of a report. Attachments and appendices can be used to further detail any terminology, findings, or recommendations presented in the report. Attachments are helpful for readers to know what they are looking at. The following may also be considered as attachments:

- Metadata
- Signature analysis file
- Evidence
- Curriculum vitae of the witnesses
- Earlier reports for reference

Including Metadata

Metadata is information about a file, including the creator of the file and time and date stamps for when the file was created and last modified. The accessibility of metadata depends on the file type. A single document can have hundreds of metadata fields, depending on the application that created the file. The following are the types of file metadata that can be used during a forensic investigation:

- *System metadata*: This type of metadata is stored outside the file and identifies the location of a file. It also includes information about filenames, dates, locations, sizes, and so on.
- *Application metadata*: This type of metadata can be stored inside the file and is used to identify changes, document author, document version, macros, e-mail information, and so on. The type of information stored varies depending on the type of the file. This type of metadata moves with the file when it is copied.

Signature Analysis

Signature analysis can be used to identify whether any files have been renamed. Most graphics and text files have a few bytes at the beginning of the file that can be used to identify the signature of a file. This signature can be used to verify that the file extension matches the file type. Both the EnCase tool and the Forensic Toolkit verify the signature of each file according to a list of known file signatures and their relevant extensions. They notify the investigator if a user has renamed a file with an extension that doesn't match the file's type.

Sample Investigative Report

Figure 6-1 shows a sample investigative report.

Case brief 1 report

REPORT OF MEDIA ANALYSIS

MEMORANDUM FOR:	County Sheriff's Police Investigator Johnson Anytown, USA 01234
SUBJECT:	Forensic Media Analysis Report SUBJECT: DOE, JOHN Case Number: 012345

1. Status: Closed.

2. Summary of Findings:

- 327 files containing images of what appeared to be children depicted in a sexually explicit manner were recovered.

- 34 shortcut files that pointed to files on floppy disks with sexually explicit file names involving children were recovered.

3. Items Analyzed:

TAG NUMBER:	**ITEM DESCRIPTION:**
012345	One Generic laptop, Serial # 123456789

4. Details of Findings:

- Findings in this paragraph related to the Generic Hard Drive, Model ABCDE, Serial # 3456ABCD, recovered from Tag Number 012345, One Generic laptop, Serial # 123456789.

  1) The examined hard drive was found to contain a Microsoft® Windows® 98 operating system.

  2) The directory and file listing for the media was saved to the Microsoft® Access Database TAG012345.MDB.

  3) The directory C:\JOHN DOE\PERSONAL\FAV PICS\, was found to contain 327 files containing images of what appeared to be children depicted in a sexually explicit manner. The file directory for 327 files disclosed that the files' creation date and times are 5 July 2001 between 11:33 p.m. and 11:45 p.m., and the last access date for 326 files listed is 27 December 2001. In addition, the file directory information for one file disclosed the last access date as 6 January 2002.

  4) The directory C:\JOHN DOE\PERSONAL\FAV PICS TO DISK\ contained 34 shortcut files that pointed to files on floppy disks with sexually explicit file names involving children. The file directory information for the 34 shortcut files disclosed the files' creation date and times are 5 July 2001 between 11:23 p.m. and 11:57 p.m., and the last access date for the 34 shortcut files was listed as 5 July 2001.

  5) The directory C:\JOHN DOE\LEGAL\ contained five Microsoft® Word documents related to various contract relationships John Doe Roofing had with other entities.

  6) The directory C:\JOHN DOE\JOHN DOE ROOFING\ contained files related to operation of John Doe Roofing.

  7) No further user-created files were present on the media.

5. Glossary:

Shortcut File: A file created that links to another file.

6. Items Provided: In addition to this hard copy report, one compact disk (CD) was submitted with an electronic copy of this report. The report on CD contains hyperlinks to the above-mentioned files and directories.

IMA D. EXAMINER Computer Forensic Examiner	Released by_____

Figure 6-1   This sample shows all of the elements that should be in an investigative report.   (*continues*)

Case brief 2

A concerned citizen contacted the police department regarding possible stolen property. He told police that while he was searching the Internet, hoping to find a motorcycle for a reasonable price, he found an ad that met his requirements. This ad listed a Honda motorcycle for a low price, so he contacted the seller. Upon meeting the seller he became suspicious that the motorcycle was stolen. After hearing this information, police started the Auto Theft Unit. The Auto Theft Unit conducted a sting operation to purchase the motorcycle. Undercover officers met with the suspect, who, after receiving payment, provided them with the vehicle, a vehicle title, registration card, and insurance card. The suspect was arrested and the vehicle he was driving was searched incident to his arrest. During the search, a notebook computer was seized. Although the documents provided by the suspect looked authentic, document examiners determined that the documents were counterfeit. The auto theft investigator contacted the computer forensic laboratory for assistance in examining the seized computer. The investigator obtained a search warrant to analyze the computer and search for materials used in making counterfeit documents and other evidence related to the auto theft charges. The laptop computer was submitted to the computer forensic laboratory for analysis.

Objective: Determine if the suspect used the laptop computer as an instrument of the crimes of Auto Theft, Fraud, Forgery, Uttering False Documents, and Possession of Counterfeit Vehicle Titles and/or as a repository of data related to those crimes.

Computer type: Gateway Solo® 9100 notebook computer.

Operating system: Microsoft® Windows® 98.

Offenses: Auto Theft, Fraud, Forgery, Uttering False Documents, and Possession of Counterfeit Vehicle Titles.

Case agent: Auto Theft Unit Investigator.

Where examination took place: Computer Forensic Laboratory.

Tools used: Guidance Software™ EnCase®, DIGit®, Jasc Software™ Quick View Plus®, and AccessData™ Password Recovery Tool Kit™.

Processing

Assessment

1. Documentation provided by the investigator was reviewed.

   a. Legal authority was established by a search warrant obtained specifically for the examination of the computer in a laboratory setting.

   b. Chain of custody was properly documented on the appropriate departmental forms.

   c. The request for service and a detailed summary explained the investigation, provided keyword lists, and provided information about the suspect, the stolen vehicle, the counterfeit documents, and the Internet advertisement. The investigator also provided photocopies of the counterfeit documents.

2. The computer forensic investigator met with the case agent and discussed additional investigative avenues and potential evidence being sought in the investigation.

3. Evidence intake was completed.

   a. The evidence was marked and photographed.

   b. A file was created and the case information was entered into the laboratory database.

   c. The computer was stored in the laboratory's property room.

4. The case was assigned to a computer forensic investigator.

Imaging

1. The notebook computer was examined and photographed.

   a. The hardware was examined and documented.

   b. A controlled boot disk was placed in the computer's floppy drive. The computer was powered on and the BIOS setup program was entered. The BIOS information was documented and the system time was compared to a trusted time source and documented. The boot sequence was checked and documented; the system was already set to boot from the floppy drive first.

   c. The notebook computer was powered off without making any changes to the BIOS.

2. EnCase® was used to create an evidence file containing the image of the notebook computer's hard drive.

   a. The notebook computer was connected to a laboratory computer through a null-modem cable, which connected to the computers' parallel ports.

   b. The notebook computer was booted to the DOS prompt with a controlled boot disk and EnCase® was started in server mode.

   c. The laboratory computer, equipped with a magneto-optical drive for file storage, was booted to the DOS prompt with a controlled boot disk. EnCase® was started in server mode and evidence files for the notebook computer were acquired and written to magneto-optical disks.

   d. When the imaging process was completed, the computers were powered off.

     i. The notebook computer was returned to the laboratory property room.

     ii. The magneto-optical disks containing the EnCase® evidence files were write-protected and entered into evidence.

Analysis

1. A laboratory computer was prepared with Windows® 98, EnCase® for Windows, and other forensic software programs.

2. The EnCase® evidence files from the notebook computer were copied to the laboratory computer's hard drive.

3. A new EnCase® case file was opened and the notebook computer's evidence files were examined using EnCase®.

   a. Deleted files were recovered by EnCase®.

   b. File data, including file names, dates and times, physical and logical size, and complete path, were recorded.

   c. Keyword text searches were conducted based on information provided by the investigator. All hits were reviewed.

   d. Graphics files were opened and viewed.

   e. HTML files were opened and viewed.

   f. Data files were opened and viewed; two password-protected and encrypted files were located.

   g. Unallocated and slack space were searched.

   h. Files of evidentiary value or investigative interest were copied/unerased from the EnCase® evidence file and copied to a compact disk.

4. Unallocated clusters were copied/unerased from the EnCase® evidence file to a clean hard drive, wiped to U.S. Department of Defense recommendations (DoD 5200.28-STD). DIGit® was then used to carve images from unallocated space. The carved images were extracted from DIGit®, opened, and viewed. A total of 6,476 images were extracted.

5. The password-protected files were copied/unerased to a 1.44 MB floppy disk. AccessData™ Password Recovery Tool Kit™ was run on the files and passwords were recovered for both files. The files were opened using the passwords and viewed.

Findings

The analysis of the notebook computer resulted in the recovery of 176 files of evidentiary value or investigative interest. The recovered files included:

1. 59 document files including documents containing the suspect's name and personal information; text included in the counterfeit documents; scanned payroll, corporate, and certified checks; text concerning and describing stolen items; and text describing the recovered motorcycle.

2. 38 graphics files including high-resolution image files depicting payroll, corporate, and certified checks; U.S. currency; vehicle titles; registration cards and driver's license templates from Georgia and other States; insurance cards from various companies; and counterfeit certified checks payable to a computer company ranging from $25,000 to $40,000 for the purchase of notebook computers. Most graphics were scanned.

3. 63 HTML files including Hotmail® and Yahoo® e-mail and classified advertisements for the recovered motorcycle, other vehicles, and several brands of notebook computers; e-mail text, including e-mails between the suspect and the concerned citizen concerning the sale of the recovered motorcycle; and e-mails between the suspect and a computer company concerning the purchase of notebook computers.

4. 14 graphics files carved from unallocated space depicting checks at various stages of completion and scanned images of U.S. currency.

5. Two password-protected and encrypted files.

   a. WordPerfect® document containing a list of personal information on several individuals including names, addresses, dates of birth, credit card and bank account numbers and expiration dates, checking account information, and other information. Password [someonesecrets].

   b. Microsoft® Word document containing vehicle title information for the recovered motorcycle. Password [HELLO].

Documentation

1. Forensic Report – All actions, processes, and findings were described in a detailed Forensic Report, which is maintained in the laboratory case file.

2. Police Report – The case agent was provided with a police report describing the evidence examined, techniques used, and the findings.

3. Work Product – A compact disk containing files and file data of evidentiary value or investigative interest was created. The original was stored in the laboratory case file. Copies were provided to the case agent and the prosecutor.

Summary

Based on the information revealed by the computer analysis, several new avenues of investigation were opened.

✔ By contacting the victims listed in the password-protected WordPerfect® document, investigators learned that the victims had all been robbed in the same city during the previous summer by an individual meeting the description of the suspect.

✔ Contact with the computer company revealed the counterfeit checks found on the suspect's computer had been accepted for the purchase of computers, and that the computers were shipped to him and were the subject of an ongoing investigation. Model numbers and serial numbers provided by the computer company matched several of the Hotmail® and Yahoo® classified ads found on the suspect's computer.

✔ Several of the counterfeit checks found on the suspect's computer were already the subject of ongoing investigations.

✔ Information recovered concerning other vehicles led to the recovery of additional stolen vehicles.

✔ The specific information sought in the search warrant concerning the sale of the stolen motorcycle and the counterfeit documents was recovered from the suspect's computer.

Conclusion

The suspect eventually plead guilty and is now incarcerated.

Figure 6-1 This sample shows all of the elements that should be in an investigative report.

(*continues*)

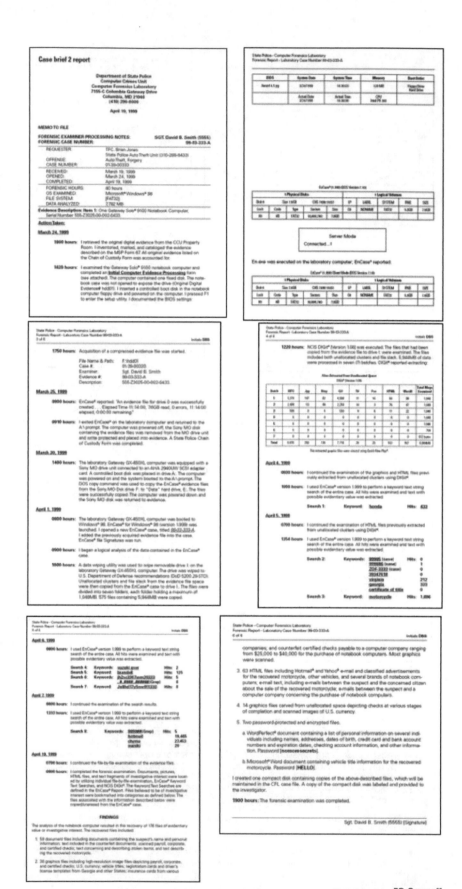

Figure 6-1 This sample shows all of the elements that should be in an investigative report.

Collecting Evidence

The investigator should collect the following types of evidence:

- *General evidence*: This includes the date and time the investigator visited the incident site and with whom the investigator spoke.
- *Physical and demonstrative evidence*: This includes pictures taken at the incident site. The investigator can demonstrate the evidence using maps, X-rays, diagrams, and floor plans.
- *Testimonial evidence*: This is oral evidence, presented by a competent eyewitness to the incident, that is relevant and material to the case. It includes testimony from all the persons interviewed by the investigator in order of the date and time of the interview.

Collecting Physical and Demonstrative Evidence

The following information should be collected for physical and demonstrative evidence:

- The manner in which the scene of the incident was secured
- A list of each type of physical evidence that was collected and secured
- The manner in which the physical evidence was collected and logged
- The manner in which the physical evidence was preserved after collection to maintain the chain of custody
- A list of any pictures that were taken
- A list of any demonstrative evidence available to the investigation

Collecting Testimonial Evidence

The following information should be collected for testimonial evidence:

- The manner in which the investigator determined whom to interview
- A list of the persons interviewed in chronological order, including the name, title, date, and time of each interview
- A list of persons who are identified as the targets of the case
- The manner in which the investigator afforded the target or the witnesses any right to representation

Dos and Don'ts of Forensic Computer Investigations

- Ask questions
- Document thoroughly
- Operate in good faith
- Do not get in over your head
- Make the decision to investigate
- Treat everything as confidential
- File everything appropriately

Case Report Writing and Documentation

All conclusions and findings of computer media analysis should go into an investigative analysis report, which is then directly sent to a case officer.

This report should have the following documents:

- Forms
- Analysis notes
- Items that come as a result of analysis, i.e., printouts and CDs
- Copies of search warrants

- Evidence listing
- Media analysis worksheet
- Keyword lists
- Support requests

Creating a Report to Attach to the Media Analysis Worksheet

An investigator should maintain notes and provide more information on the following to create a report that can be attached to the media analysis worksheet:

- Date and time when any computer taken as evidence
- Current date and time
- Lapses in analysis
- Finding evidence
- Special techniques required that are beyond the normal processes
- Significant problems or broken items
- Outside sources that provide assistance during the investigation

Best Practices for Investigators

Before submitting the final report, an investigator should read it over to see if there are any places where he or she needs to make changes. The report should contain only relevant material. It should also be coherent, not repetitive, and consistently structured. The investigator should also let an outsider read the report. The report needs to be understandable to someone who is completely unfamiliar with the case.

Writing a Report Using FTK

To prepare a new case using FTK, perform the following steps:

1. Write-protect the evidence floppy disk.
2. Create a work folder and another folder under this folder.
3. Run FTK.
4. Click **OK**.
5. Select **Start a new case** and click **OK** in the **FTK Startup** dialog box (Figure 6-2).
6. Fill out the appropriate information in the **New Case** dialog box and click **Continue**.
7. Use the **Browse** button to access the case path.

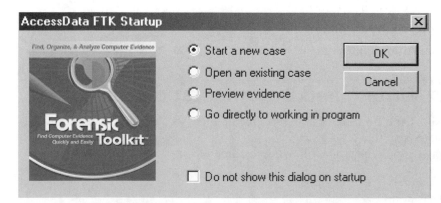

Figure 6-2   Select **Start a new case** in the **FTK Startup** dialog box.

8. Give a brief description of the investigation (Figure 6-3) and click **Next**.

9. Check all the boxes in the **Case Log Options** window (Figure 6-4).

10. Click **Next** in the **Evidence Processing Options** window (Figure 6-5).

11. Click **Next** in the **Refine Case and Refine Index** window.

12. In the **Add Evidence to Case** window (Figure 6-6), click the **Add Evidence** button.

13. The **Add Evidence to Case** dialog box appears. Click the **Local Drive** option and then click **Continue**.

14. Select the **A: drive** option and the **Logical option** button in the **Select Local Drive** dialog box, and click **OK**.

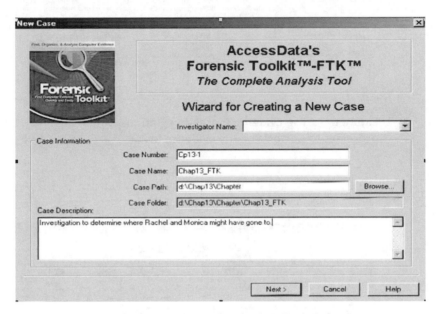

Figure 6-3   The case description should be brief but informative.

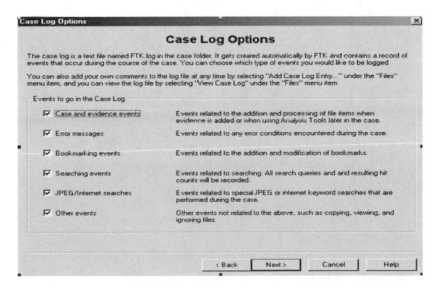

Figure 6-4   The **Case Log Options** window lets a user choose what to include in the case log.

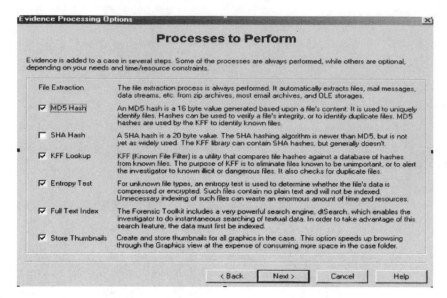

Figure 6-5   The **Evidence Processing Options** window tells FTK which processes to perform on the evidence files.

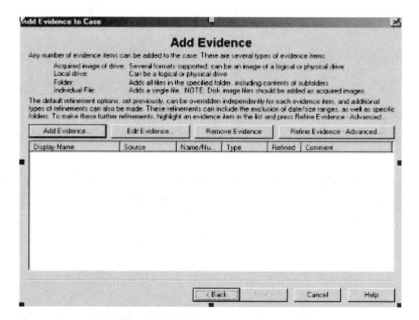

Figure 6-6   Click the **Add Evidence** button to add evidence.

15. Enter comments in the **Evidence Information** window (Figure 6-7) and then click **OK.**

16. Click **Next** in the **Add Evidence** window.

17. Check the information in the **Case Summary** window (Figure 6-8). If it is correct, click **Finish.** Otherwise, click **Back** to fix any errors.

FTK starts analyzing the data on the investigation floppy disk when the FTK **Processing Files** window (Figure 6-9) appears. When FTK completes the analysis, the main FTK window (Figure 6-10) appears showing all data found from the analysis process.

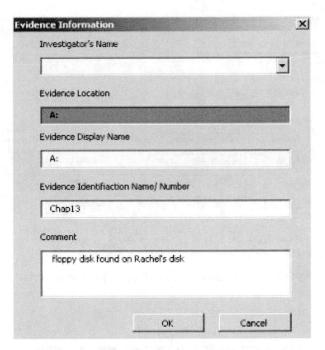

Figure 6-7 Enter a comment that describes the evidence.

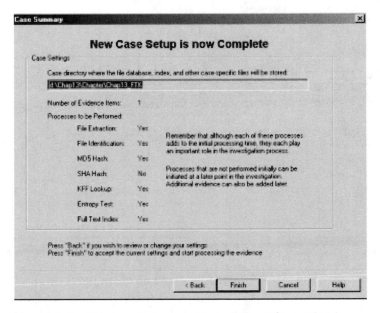

Figure 6-8 Check to make sure that all the information in this window is correct before moving on.

Analyzing with FTK

Perform the following steps to collect pictures with FTK:

1. Click the **Graphics** tab and check the **List all descendants** box.

2. Click any picture in the upper pane (Figure 6-11) and check the box next to its filename.

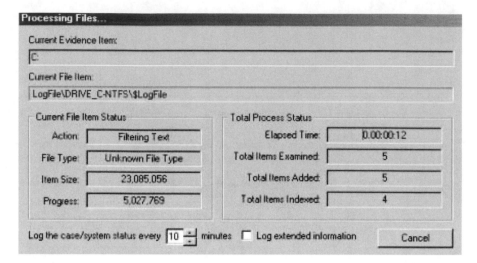

Figure 6-9 This screen shows FTK's progress in processing the evidence files.

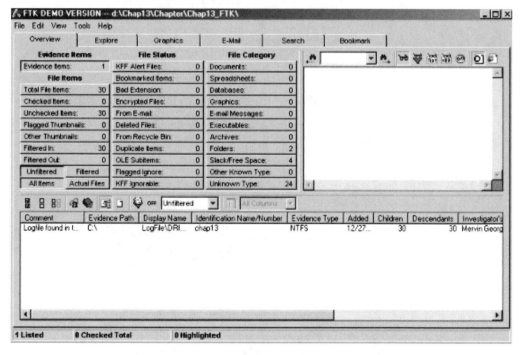

Figure 6-10 The main FTK window shows all of the processed evidence files.

Locating Encrypted Files with FTK

To locate encrypted files with FTK, click the **Overview** tab, click the **Encrypted Files** button (Figure 6-12), and click any file in the lower pane.

Viewing Encrypted Files

After locating the encrypted files, perform the following steps to view them:

1. Check the box next to the clicked file.
2. Right-click the file and click **Export File** on the shortcut menu.

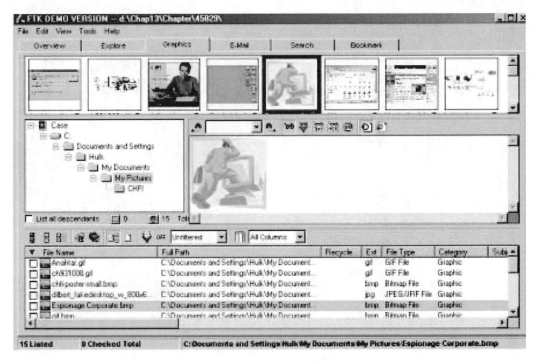

Figure 6-11   Users can analyze graphics files with FTK.

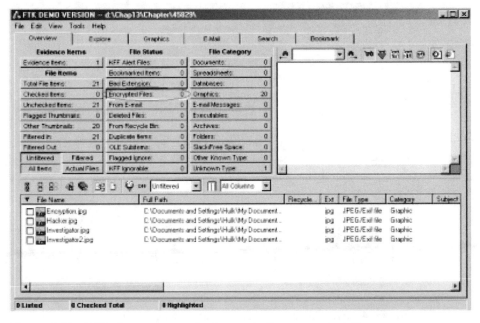

Figure 6-12   FTK allows users to look at only the encrypted files.

3. Uncheck all boxes located at the bottom of the **Export Files** dialog box (Figure 6-13) and click **OK**.

4. Click **OK** in the **Export Files** window message.

Searching with FTK

Perform the following steps to execute an indexed search:

1. Click the **Search** tab.

2. Type the first search term in the **Search Term** field and click **Add**.

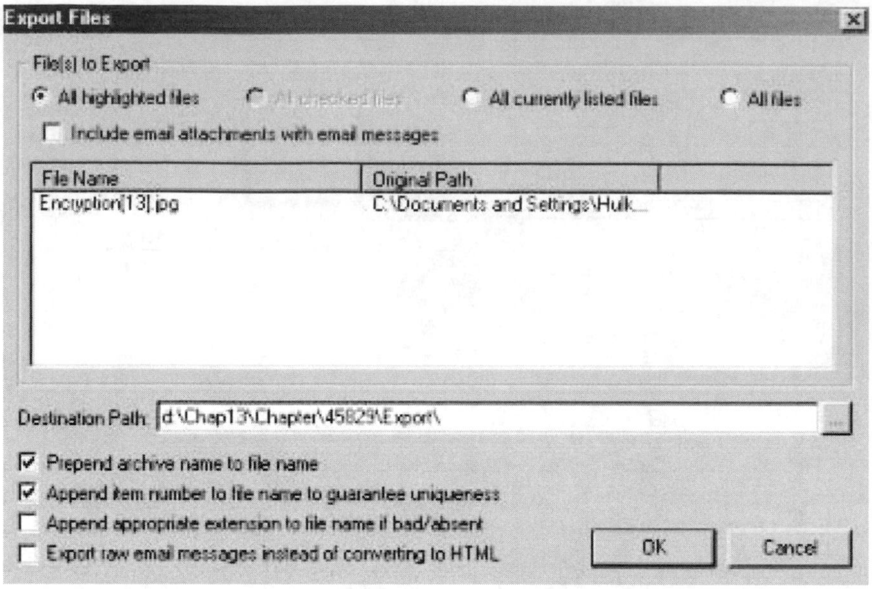

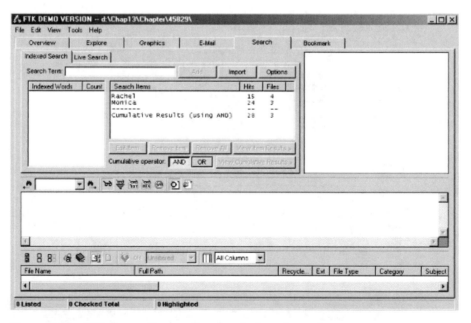

Figure 6-13   FTK allows users to export encrypted files for later viewing.

Figure 6-14   FTK shows the results of an indexed search.

3. Then type another search term and click **Add**.

4. Click **View Cumulative Results**. You will see a window like Figure 6-14.

Perform the following steps to execute a live search:

1. Click the **Live Search** tab in the **Search** pane (Figure 6-15).

2. Type a keyword and click **Add**. Click **Search**, and then click **OK** in the **Retrieve Search Hits** dialog box.

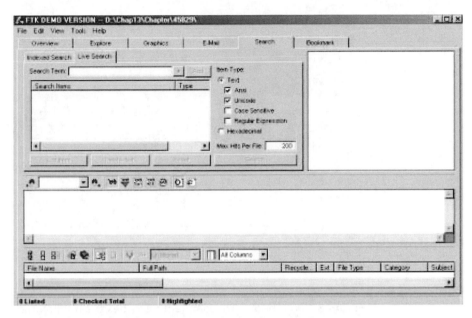

Figure 6-15   FTK allows users to perform a live search.

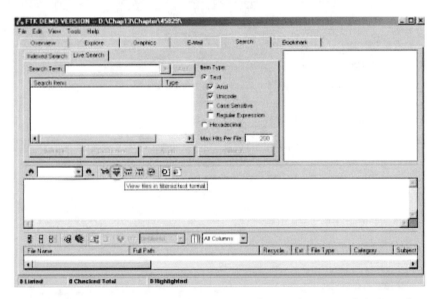

Figure 6-16   The **View files in filtered text format** button minimizes the data.

3. Click **View Results** in the **Live Search Progress** dialog box.

4. To minimize the data, click the **View files in filtered text format** icon (Figure 6-16).

Creating a Bookmark for Investigation Findings

Perform the following steps to create a bookmark for investigation findings:

1. Right-click any checked file and then click **Create Bookmark** on the shortcut menu.

2. Type **ch13_search_results** in the **Bookmark name** text box. Click **All checked items,** and then check **Include in report** and **Export files** in the **Create New Bookmark** dialog box.

3. To describe the bookmark, type a comment (Figure 6-17) and then click **OK**.

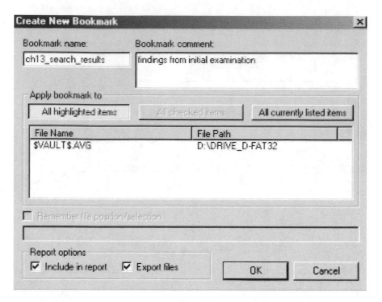

Figure 6-17 A bookmark comment describes the bookmark.

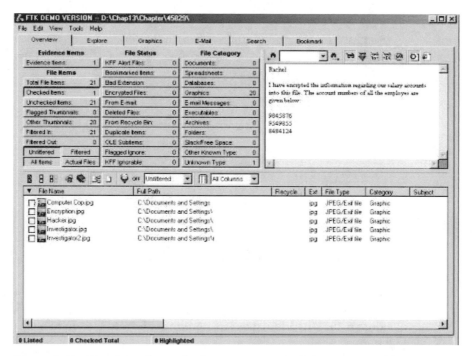

Figure 6-18 The **Overview** tab gives a summary of the evidence files in the case.

Reviewing Case Findings in FTK

To review case findings in FTK, click the **Overview** tab (Figure 6-18) and then click the **Checked Items** button.

Viewing Selected Items

To view selected items, perform the following steps:

1. Click the first file in the lower pane.
2. The contents of the bookmark can be read by scrolling down the upper-right pane (Figure 6-19).

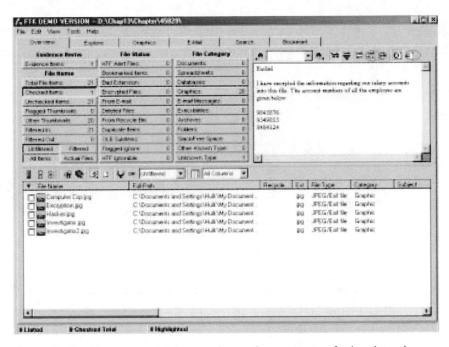

Figure 6-19 The upper-right pane shows the contents of a bookmark.

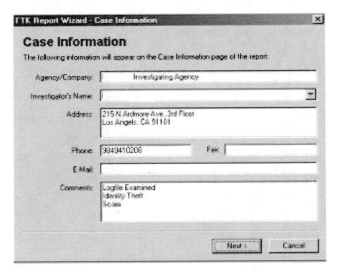

Figure 6-20 Enter information about the case in the
Case Information window.

3. Type the keyword value in the search text box to locate a specific keyword that is displayed in the upper-right pane.

4. To view graphic files, click the **Internet Explorer** icon located above the upper-right pane.

5. To view binary files, click the **HEX** icon.

Running the FTK Report Wizard

1. Go to **File** in the main FTK window and then click **Report Wizard**.

2. Enter the appropriate information in the **Case Information** window (Figure 6-20). Click **Next**.

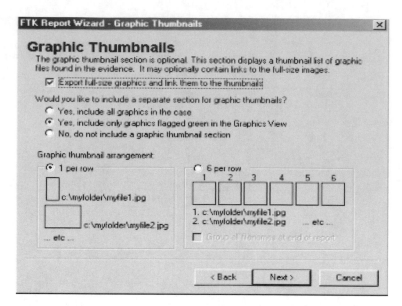

Figure 6-21   Users can choose whether to add graphic thumbnails to the report.

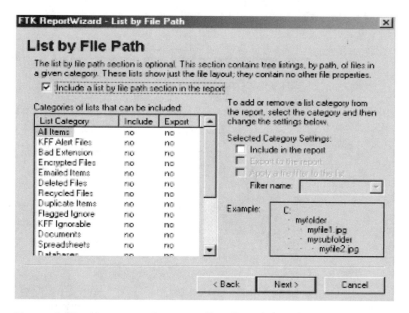

Figure 6-22   Users can choose to list all evidence files in the report.

3. Click **Next** on both the **Bookmarks – A** and **Bookmarks – B** dialog boxes.

4. In the **Graphic Thumbnails** dialog box (Figure 6-21), check **Export full-size graphics and link them to the thumbnails** and then click **Next**.

5. In the **List by File Path** dialog box (Figure 6-22), check the **Include a list by file path section in the report** box. Also check the **Include in the report** and **Export to the report** boxes and then click **Next**.

6. In the **Case Audit Files** dialog box, click **Add Files** and navigate to the chap13chapter folder.

7. In the **Open** dialog box, press and hold down the **Ctrl** key to select all the evidence files and then click **Open**.

8. Click **Next** in the **Case Audit Files** dialog box.

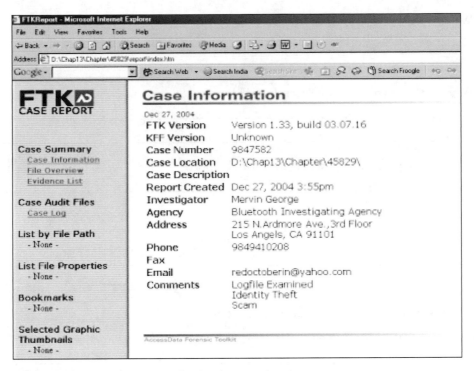

Figure 6-23   Users can view the final report in a browser.

9. Click **Finish** in the **Report Location** dialog box.
10. Click **Yes** to view the report generated. The report opens in Windows Explorer. Double-click Index.html in the chap13chap13_FTKReport folder to view the report in Internet Explorer (Figure 6-23).

Chapter Summary

- Reports can be used to communicate the results of a forensic investigation. They can be used not only to present the facts but also to communicate expert opinions.
- Reports can be formal or informal, verbal or written.
- It is essential for anyone writing a formal report to pay attention to word usage, grammar, spelling, and details.
- Avoid usage of jargon, slang, or colloquial terms when writing a report.
- Reports should include results and conclusions.
- The final product that can be shown to the attorney or client is a combination of reports generated using forensic tools and official investigative reports.

Review Questions

1. What is an investigative report?

_____

_____

2. What is the purpose of a verbal formal report?

_____

_____

3. What is the purpose of a verbal informal report?

_____

_____

4. What is the purpose of a written formal report?

_____

_____

5. What is the purpose of a written informal report?

_____

_____

6. Name four examples of demonstrative evidence.

_____

_____

7. What is the purpose of appendices to a report?

_____

_____

8. What is the purpose of supporting material in a report?

_____

_____

Hands-On Projects

1. Perform the following steps:
   - Navigate to Chapter 6 of the Student Resource Center.
   - Read Incident-Investigation Report Requirements.pdf.
2. Perform the following steps:
   - Navigate to Chapter 6 of the Student Resource Center.
   - Read planning to write report.pdf.
3. Perform the following steps:
   - Navigate to Chapter 6 of the Student Resource Center.
   - Read Writing investigation report.pdf.

Index